HEALING
FOR LEADERSHIP

HOW EMOTIONALLY INTELLIGENT LEADERS BUILD SAFE, RESILIENT TEAMS

DR. ANTOINETTE GUTIERREZ

Healing For Leadership: How Emotionally Intelligent Leaders Build Safe, Resilient Teams

Publicity Rights

For information on publicity, author interviews, presentation, and subsidiary rights, contact:

Dr. Marilou Ryder: drmlr@yahoo.com 760-900-0556

Dr. Antoinette Gutierrez: gtzleadershipconsulting@gmail.com 619-992-5190

DELMAR
PUBLISHING

REVIEWS

"*Healing for Leadership* highlights the importance of connection, self-awareness, and relational management in educational leadership, advocating for a shift from traditional management to a healing-centered approach. The book emphasizes that great leaders are remembered for how they make others feel—valued, supported, and trusted—rather than just their expertise. Practical strategies for fostering understanding, managing relationships, and maintaining clear communication make this a valuable guide for educators."

~Lori Leyden, PhD, Trauma Healing Expert,
Evolutionary Leaders Council Member

✻

"*Healing for Leadership* will be invaluable for any leader in today's fast-paced and high-pressure world of education and business. As a very involved parent in my children's education and someone who has worked with schools and other parents for years, I highly recommend this book. The explanations of what a ' trauma-informed' approach is and why it is so important are excellent."

~Robert MacPhee, Founder,
Excellent Decisions Leadership,
Author of Living a Values Based Life

Healing for Leadership is a practical guide to the necessary personal inner work that every leader needs to complete to effectively lead people in today's world. It provides the important pre-work that needs to be done before working on the external leadership skills that most leadership books only focus on. Although illustrated with vignettes drawn from the world of education, the skills and processes covered can be applied by any leader at any level of any organization. I highly recommend it.

~Jack Canfield,
Coauthor of the Chicken Soup for the Soul® series
and The Success Principles™, and Founder of the
Transformational Leadership Council

CONTENTS

Reviews   *iii*

Author's Note   *vi*

Acknowledgements   *vii*

Introduction: Healing Leaders   1

1. Power of Connection   18

2. Trauma Responses in Education   35

3. Self Awareness   50

4. Managing Your Emotional State   60

5. Trauma: Understanding Others   71

6. Managing Relationships   85

7. Bringing it All Together   98

8. Other Tips for Successful Healing Leadership   103

Adverse Childhood Experience Questionnaire   *114*

How Established Culture Plays a Role in Recovering

from Staffing Shortages   *116*

References   *122*

About the Author   *125*

Author's Note

To be clear, this is a book for all humans who want to show up for others. The stories included are my own, primarily focused on educational leadership. Still, the concepts and strategies can be applied by all leaders who want to show up to help others heal. The ideas and strategies are applicable to any position across any industry. If you are interested in being a better version of yourself or always wonder how those amazing leaders you have had achieved their way of being, this book is for you. If you are already showing up for others but sometimes feel disappointed in your own reactions to new situations, this book is for you. If you've picked up this book and are reading it right now, it's meant for you. Heal so you can help others heal so that we can be amazing together.

Love,
Dr G

Acknowledgements

I want to acknowledge, first and foremost, my family for allowing me to explore and express who I really am throughout the many stages of my life, which took me away from them to care for others.

Over the years, I have had many teachers and mentors, both official and unofficial. My first leadership idol was Dennis Payne, who taught me how to treat people and de-escalate situations without giving in to their demands, but rather by listening and being present.

My second was Brian Wood, who hired me as a teacher from industry and who immediately saw leadership in me in education and my second year, made me a department chair. He saw something I did not and set me on a trajectory of leadership as well as strategic thinking. He had a knack for placing the right people in the right positions.

The third was Dr. Beatrice Gray, who taught me that I had to trust and protect those in my care so they could do their job. Developing people and trusting them was more important than completing tasks. This lesson established the foundation of my educational leadership.

Fourth was Dr. Marilyn Saucedo, a small but mighty southern Cuban high school principal who taught me bravery and the benefits and costs of doing the right thing. She taught me that I needed to act on what I believed was right for both students and staff, and how to support them. She also set me on my path to a doctoral degree.

Finally, I want to thank Dr. Dale Marsden, who demonstrated leadership through crisis, maintaining calm in the face of chaos, and collaborative leadership, as well as what it means to develop and trust the adults in the system to do right by kids.

Introduction: Healing Leaders

Leading yourself and others through trauma in education.
"You can love people without leading them, but you cannot
lead people without loving them."
                    ~John Maxwell[1]

L et's start with an understanding of the title. What does it mean to lead with healing in mind? In a world where stress, trauma, burnout, and disconnection are rampant in our organizations, leaders must evolve beyond managing tasks. Leaders must be human-centered in their approach, demonstrating equal mastery of both human understanding and instructional expertise. *Healing for Leadership* explores what it takes to heal yourself so you can show up as the best leader you can be, as well as to create a healing space for others to thrive in their work.

What do great leaders do to make their teams feel truly cared for? In this chapter, you'll discover seven powerful behaviors shared by top leaders across healthcare, law enforcement, education, and business, straight from the voices of those who work alongside them every day.

Every great leadership book and book about excellent teaching begins with relationships, relationships, relationships. That sounds so simple, and yet it is not simple at all when it comes to connecting with and making every single person feel valued. People are complex, with thousands of human variations of experiences that create who we are and what we are about.

Within that, we also all have triggers and beliefs that shape how we see the world, others, and especially our "bosses" and "leaders." While writing this book, I asked people across all levels of education and various industries to share a time when they felt truly loved and cared for by a leader, whether through writing or conversation. What was the situation? How did you feel? And what did the leader do to make you feel that way?" Here are a few statements from fields outside education.

"A good leader inspires others and creates a vision that draws buy-in and ties to the big picture. They build capacity with intention, trust their team to make strong decisions, and strive to build contingency so the work always continues with purpose and momentum."

~Scott Raine, former Starbucks District Manager

"Effective leadership means fostering a team that treats every patient with compassion and dignity. Emphasizing the importance of cultural respect, empathy, and recognizing that behind every prescription is a person who may be facing unseen challenges. This not only improves patient care but also helps everyone on the team grow and succeed in their healthcare careers."

~James Hattar, Pharmacy Manager

"After retiring from a twenty-five-year career in law enforcement and transitioning to a new career in education, I believe that leadership in law enforcement is grounded in integrity, accountability, and a commitment to serving others. A good leader in these fields sets the tone through their actions, leading by example with honesty, fairness, and empathy. In law enforcement, strong leadership means making sound decisions under pressure, building trust within the community, and fostering a culture of professionalism and respect among officers. In education, it involves inspiring staff and students, creating a safe and inclusive learning environment, and being a visionary who champions growth and innovation. In both careers, the best leaders are those who listen actively, communicate clearly, and empower others to reach their full potential while always putting service and ethics at the forefront."

~DJ Jones, Teacher, former Parole Officer

Angelo Flores, a former VP at Bank of America, submitted this last story. Instead of submitting a partial quote, I wanted to include the story in its entirety because this story exemplifies the behavior that is repeatedly displayed by leaders who make their team feel seen and heard.

"Walking into the building for an interview, I came across a gentleman who greeted me as he proceeded to dump trash from smaller trash cans into a larger rolling bin.

I thought it was odd for a janitor to be dressed so nicely but I figured a janitor working at a Fortune 500 company should have higher standards. Walking to the parking lot after my interview, I noticed the same gentleman, now without his coat and tie, tossing several industrial-sized trash bags into the trash bins. This time, the shine of his shoes caught my eye... I wondered why a Janitor would be wearing such expensive shoes? The gentleman paused to toss the bags, waving goodbye and wishing me the best of luck.

Turns out, luck was on my side; I got the job.

Not long after, I learned something that left me stunned. The man I thought was a janitor wasn't a janitor at all; he was the highest-ranking executive at the corporate office.

At first, I was baffled. However, as time passed, I noticed a pattern. Every interaction was always thoughtful, sincere, and warm. He wanted to know more about me as a person, not just as "the employee," always including a thank you for a specific contribution or project I had worked on. It always left me feeling valued and understood. He made everyone feel that way.

As I grew in my career, he was always one of the first to congratulate me. "Keep going," he would say. "The sky's the limit." No matter how busy, he always lent an ear, offering genuine advice and sometimes some hard-to-swallow criticism. He was a true mentor. As time went on, my departments and teams were consistently among the top in the nation. Eventually, I became one of the top VPs at the site, winning multiple national awards, including a prestigious, peer-nominated honor.

So, what's the secret of leading successfully? There isn't one. Nor is there a quick "how to" guide to follow. It's simple. Take the time to genuinely get to know the person you lead. Be sincere and intentional. Learn what they do, regardless of the project's size or the task's complexity. And always, always say thank you.

And as for that moment, the one that stuck with me all these years, you might still be wondering: Why was the executive picking up trash?

That day, a part-time janitor had to leave suddenly. His wife was undergoing an emergency C-section. Learning what had happened, the Executive stepped in without hesitation to cover his shift.

What most didn't know was that the Janitor and his wife had been trying to get pregnant for years. He took on this part-time job in addition to his full-time job to help cover the cost of in vitro fertilization. The Executive had taken the time to learn this, just as he took the time to learn about all of us."

~Angelo Flores, Former Bank of America VP

The professionals who shared their stories described leaders who believed in them, trusted them, respected them, loved them, empathized with them, understood them, and made them feel truly valued. But what does that look like? Several powerful themes and behaviors surfaced through their heartfelt responses.

As leaders, we all want the people we serve to feel trusted, loved, and respected at their workplace and safe with those in charge. It would be a very short book if all I did were tell leaders to 'trust' or 'value' their employees. We recognize that these concepts are important, and extensive research supports them, as outlined in "The Speed of Trust" by Stephen M. R. Covey. But I wanted to dig deeper. I wanted to know what, specifically, those leaders did to make people feel trusted, valued, and genuinely cared for.

The behaviors and actions outlined in this chapter are practical steps that anyone can take. While some may overlap, I've listed them separately to emphasize the different paths individuals can take to reach the same goal, understanding that what works may vary from person to person. The actions are presented in order of how frequently they were mentioned, from most to least.

Recognition

The most frequently shared action was recognition. Some of these actions ranged from a simple verbal "good job" to small gifts of recognition, such as flowers, to more formal recognition, including award nominations.

Allowed Mistakes

The second most mentioned was their leader creating a safe space for mistakes or trying new things. One leader said, "Nothing you can do will burn down the school," alleviating the pressure of perfection. Another supported their teacher in proposing ideas and being supported in trying them if there was a logical reason for it.

Teaching/Coaching

The comments went beyond simply being taught something by a leader. They reflected a deeper level of care and investment. These leaders took the time to develop their team members' skills, recognizing their potential and offering personalized support through mentorship. This action often included thoughtful follow-up with targeted feedback or recommending specific training opportunities they knew would help that individual grow.

Listen/Be Available

The participants felt heard. They had leaders who ensured they were accessible, listened to, and provided appropriate help, whether through cognitive coaching to help the person come up with their own solution, by listening and holding time and space, or by resolving the issue. The leaders were not listening to respond but truly listening.

Gave Freedom

Freedom is tied to trust. The respondents, ranging from teachers to higher-level administrators, were free to try out their ideas and/or speak up in meetings. They may have helped them craft it with some questions, but they gave them the trust to do the right thing for the situation.

Provided Resources

While not the most frequently mentioned form of support, this theme was consistently mentioned. Leaders found meaningful ways to provide what their team members needed, whether it was time, funding, or tangible resources, to help them succeed.

Taking and Giving Time

Being present matters. Most people understand how busy leaders are, often juggling responsibilities that aren't always visible. That's why it's so meaningful when a leader takes the time to be fully present without rushing, multitasking, or distractions. Examples included walking through classrooms or schools, maintaining an open-door policy, answering a call during a personal crisis, or visiting the hospital when a family member was in need. It wasn't just time, it was quality time.

Letting Them Lead

This theme is closely tied to trust, value, and allowing room for mistakes. When employees feel valued and supported, their leaders empower them by stepping back and letting them lead. Their leader allowed them to run with their ideas, encouraged various voices at the table, and not only allowed it but also supported it so that failure would not be met with an "I got you so" from their leader. Other examples also included verbal support, such as publicly backing a school or supporting their decisions in various companies.

Having Fun

Many of these leaders who created safe spaces reduced the stress and anxiety of failure by fostering a team atmosphere, and as a result, they had fun! There is always hard work, laughter, and positive shared memories. Having fun includes leaders who don't take themselves too seriously.

To master most of these skills, we, as leaders, must be present and able to manage ourselves effectively, truly seeing the people we serve and creating a safe space for them to be their authentic selves.

One leader who demonstrated these things for me was Dr. Beatrice Grey, one of my first principal bosses.

My first administrative job was as an elementary assistant principal at three different elementary schools. I had three very different leaders at very different schools with very different expectations.

The leader that stood out the most was oddly not known for warm and fuzzy relationships. Dr. Beatrice Gray was a stern leader who leaned into difficult conversations with staff, parents, and students. She saw the potential in everyone and made sure she supported them.

As a new administrator, I wanted to ensure that I was responsive to everyone who needed me, including the supervising playground staff, who frequently called me. I would run out to the playground or wherever they requested me to help with the situation.

One day, I was in her office, and a call came through on the radio. She told me to have a seat and that I needed to trust and support staff in doing their jobs, not doing their job for them, because then I am not doing mine.

This early lesson taught everyone that they were capable of doing their job, and as a leader, my role was not to take over their duties but to build people's capacity to excel in their own work. If I made a mistake, she would sit me down and we would talk through it; she would guide me by explaining my error and the reasoning behind it, so I could learn to make better decisions in the future. She made me a true thought partner, let me make my own mistakes, and supported me when I wanted to try to implement some PBIS lunch groups way before they were as widely spread as they are today. Her leadership largely influenced my leadership philosophy as I have grown.

LEAD & LEARN HIGHLIGHTS

The description of a great leader who makes people feel loved and cared about includes someone who:

* Gives recognition
* Allows mistakes
* Teaches and coaches
* Listens and is available
* Gives freedom
* Takes and gives time
* Provides resources
* Let others lead
* Has fun!

Leadership Reflection Worksheet

*Becoming a Leader Who Makes Others Feel Loved &
Appreciated*

As you reflect on what it means to be a great leader—someone who fosters a sense of care, support, and value within their team—take a few moments to think about a time when you felt loved, seen, and supported by a leader. Use the prompts below to guide your reflection.

1. Which leadership actions described in this chapter did the leader you respected consistently demonstrate? (List and explain specific actions you recall.)

_____

_____

2. Did this leader take additional actions not mentioned in this chapter? If so, what were they? (Think about unique ways they made you feel appreciated.)

_____

_____

3. Describe a situation in which this leader truly had your back. What did they do, and how did it impact you?

_____

_____

4. How did their leadership make you feel—personally and professionally?

_____

_____

5. Which of these actions do you intentionally bring into your own leadership today? (Be honest about what you do well and what you might want to improve.)

_____

_____

6. When people describe your leadership, what do you hope they say they felt? (Love, respect, trust, support?)

_____

_____

7. Would your current or former team members describe you as a great leader who made them feel loved and appreciated? Why or why not?

_____

_____

An Assessment

Unlock Your Healing Leadership Potential

Welcome to *your healing journey.* This quick self-assessment will help you evaluate your current stage in the journey to becoming a healing leader. Reflecting on these questions will provide valuable insights into the skills you are already incorporating into your daily work and identify areas for focus in your professional growth.

Directions:

Read Each Question Carefully

Consider each question in the context of your recent work experiences and career. Consider specific examples and situations that illustrate your current approach and behavior.

Choose the Response that Best Reflects Your Experience

For each question, select the response that most accurately represents how you handle the situation described or to the degree you feel you demonstrate that skill. Use the scale provided to rate yourself.

Reflect on Your Answers

Once you have completed the quiz, review your responses to identify patterns or areas where you may want to focus on improving. Pay attention to questions where you rated yourself lower, as these could be areas for potential growth.

Apply Insights to Your Leadership Strategy

Use the insights gained from this quiz to target what portion of the book you may want to pay special attention to or spend more time on. Consider how you can enhance your skills as a healing leader, and if you are already a seasoned one, how can you deepen your knowledge and applied skills?

Set Actionable Goals

Based on your reflections, set specific goals and actions to address any gaps or opportunities for improvement. Track your progress and revisit the quiz periodically to measure your growth and readiness for future challenges.

By taking this quiz, you are taking a proactive step toward unlocking your healing leadership potential and advancing your leadership career with confidence. Good luck!

		4 All of the time	3 Most of the time	2 Some- times	1 Not yet
1.	I build relationships and trust easily with those I work with.				
2.	I am able to pause when something happens and think thoughtfully about my response to it, rather than reacting emotionally.				
3.	I am highly aware of my triggers and how I respond to stress and work to counter those responses.				
4.	I take time for myself to balance the stress of my work.				
5.	I am aware of the survival responses in the body (fight, flight, freeze, or fawn) and when an employee may be exhibiting that behavior, instead of taking it personally.				
6.	I am aware of my emotions when I am in a stressful situation and can name the feeling and identify why I am feeling that way in that moment.				
7.	I can address my team with curiosity instead of anger when I implement something and there is pushback.				

		4 All of the time	3 Most of the time	2 Some-times	1 Not yet
8.	I can generally pick up unrest, worry, anger, etc, in my team before they have to tell me.				
9.	I am able to navigate emotionally charged topics with a group with ease.				
10.	I am able to be authentic in my everyday dealings with my team.				
11.	I regularly read, listen to podcasts, or attend professional learning sessions to continue my growth.				
12.	I have lookouts at my work who are not afraid to tell me the truth or if I make a mistake.				
13.	I approach my work regularly with a positive attitude and a sense of humor.				
14.	I love the people on my team.				
15.	I have well-established communication protocols.				
	Total Points in Each Category				

Scoring: Add the total number of points in each column.

55-60 ~ HEALER

You're already harnessing the power of creating a safe space for your team to flourish! Your self-awareness and ability to navigate people's emotions demonstrate that you are a highly caring individual who creates a healing space for others. Revisit this book when you need a reminder, and share it with a friend!

45-54 ~ ON THE LAUNCH PAD!

You're well on your way to creating a healing space. You have a solid awareness of what is happening and how you and others are feeling, but may struggle with managing those emotions regularly or just need a couple more strategies to get there. Focus on these areas, and you will be soaring to new heights in no time!

30-44 ~ TIME FOR A BOOST!

You're off to a good start. You may be aware of some strategies and have some insight into your own emotions and those of others. Identify a few key areas you would like to improve and focus on those until you feel you have started to internalize them.

1-29 ~ WELCOME TO THE JOURNEY!

You're taking the first steps towards being a healing leader. Reflect on the strategies presented in the book and take your time to engage in the deep work. Don't be afraid to pause and go through the book and reflections slowly. Consider finding an accountability partner who can give you feedback on how well you are mastering the skills. Your healing journey starts here!

Chapter 1

Power of Connection

*"Connection is the energy that exists between people
when they feel seen, heard, and valued; when they can
give and receive without judgment; and when they
derive sustenance and strength from the relationship"*

~ Brene Brown[2]

I n this chapter, you will learn the definitions and uses
of the critical terms used throughout this book, which
clarify the meanings of the words being defined, thereby
removing potential connotations associated with them. You
will also learn why this topic is more important now than
ever in our ever-changing society. Finally, this chapter will
explore the overall concept of healing for leadership, its
meaning, and why it is essential to begin with oneself.

The educational landscape has undergone a dramatic shift
since the 2020 pandemic shutdowns. With an increasingly
polarized environment seeping into the nation and local aca-
demic setting, leading our staff and students is increasingly
complex. Adding to the complexity, some of the communities we serve face ongoing challenges such as poverty and
violence. We need more leaders who can support the community in ways beyond what we originally asked for. We need
more emotionally aware leaders who can support people in all

their humanness and create and improve systems and structures. We need leaders who have been healed and can help others heal.

I am an optimistic realist (I am unsure if this is a real term). It means that I see many possibilities for what can be, but also know that to make those possibilities a reality, I must be aware of and address the reality of where we are, thereby closing the gap between reality and the wonders of future possibilities. Effective leadership today requires significantly more inner work than it did in the past, and this does not end once you leave the site and go to the district office. We need leadership in all roles and titles. In my 15 years of leadership, regardless of the role, I have learned that the more self-love and self-awareness I possess, the better I can show up for others and be the leader I strive to be.

Today, there is considerable discussion about trauma-informed practices in relation to the health and wellness of students. This focus on mental health is a fantastic shift in our world today. It even extends to discussing what teachers must teach in the classroom to provide trauma-informed teaching. One of my favorite books on this subject is Fostering Resilient Learners: Strategies for Creating a Trauma-Sensitive Classroom by authors Kristen Souers and Pete Hall (2016). The book explores the concept of trauma-sensitive teaching, which suggests that it is not essential to identify the specific trauma but rather to adopt healing behaviors for students. [*3] I love it because it gives clear and actionable steps to implement immediately. I led a book study with this book with a high school staff, chosen by the leadership team, which was also very well received.

There are even some mentions of needing trauma-informed Leadership in an article in Edutopia titled "3 tips for using trauma-informed practices as a school leader" by Brittany Collins,[*4] who gives three practical tips on creating a safe school environment. Overall, however, much of the literature focuses more on classroom strategies than on the need for leaders to possess the skills to support teachers in their emotional well-being. In this book, I would like to focus on the trauma-informed or healing leader who has the responsibility to help the adults in their care (starting with themselves). We recognize that in education, our roles are designed to serve adults, children, and young adults. But regardless of the organization, we are responsible for those we serve.

However, to serve our customers, whether students or end-users of a product, we do so through the adults who have direct contact with them on a daily basis. The more I experience the educational system as a system of humans, the more I believe in the philosophy embodied by the Richard Branson quote, "Clients do not come first. Employees come first. They will care for the clients if you care for your employees" (Branson, n.d.)[*5]. I know some people rankle with this idea, and I understand. I invite you to sit with it for a moment and evaluate what comes to mind.

The old me's first reaction was, "We are here for the kids; the adults should do their job, they are getting paid, and they should not be in the profession if they don't want to do right by kids." The current me still holds some of that belief because I believe that we have a moral obligation to be the voice for students and families who either don't know how to advocate for themselves or cannot. However, I also believe that we overlook the complexities of what adults bring with their own traumas and life experiences, as well as the challenges and needs for support to be successful in their quest to do right by students.

As an institution, we do not always practice what we believe about hope, learning, and the possibility that everyone can and wants to achieve. We generously apply these principles to students but often forget that we are leading and teaching many other adults throughout our schools, adults who were once children and have grown up, still navigating the world to the best of their ability. This begs the question: how do we serve the adults in the system with the same assumptions, care, and safe spaces as we expect them to provide for our children?

Before we begin, we must be on the same page regarding the use of everyday language. Throughout this book, we will use certain terms that I want to ensure have been explicitly defined. Below are some terms that have been used in various contexts and have multiple meanings. To provide clarity, I've included both a dictionary definition and my own interpretation of how the terms and ideas will be applied in this book.

What is trauma?

The definition from Oxford Languages defines trauma as a deeply distressing or disturbing experience.

Many of us can categorize trauma in the most severe examples we have either lived or have heard about. One well-cited research study conducted by the CDC in the mid-1990s examined the link between traumatic childhood experiences and later life health. They discovered a few "triggers" they named ACES or adverse childhood experiences, which are linked to negative health and wellness practices later in life, such as addiction and obesity. The ACES questions can be viewed in the appendix.

Most of us agree that many of these events, such as child abuse, drug or alcohol abuse, neglect, or psychological abuse, would be traumatic events. What about working for a leader who repeatedly dismisses your ideas whenever you feel brave enough to speak up? Or if something happens in the community that affects the students and staff, such as a large fire? Repeated microaggressions? Or, as a leader, a contentious board that gets bogged down in divisive politics that ignores the needs of some students? The definition seems simple on the surface. However, it implies individuality in the words used to describe it. For example, what is distressing or disturbing to one person may not be to another. Therefore, trauma is in the eye of the beholder.

The scenarios mentioned above are everyday occurrences for today's education leaders, yet they still require intentional processing and management in order to sustain a high level of healing leadership. The term trauma will be used frequently throughout this book. While we don't need to know the specific trauma behind someone's reactions in order to support them, we do need to recognize that it is a person's interpretation and internalization of an event that determines whether it is experienced as traumatic.

What is stress?

Merriam Webster Dictionary: a physical, chemical, or emotional factor that causes bodily or mental tension and may be a factor in disease causation.

For the sake of this book, both trauma and stress have many similarities and will be used interchangeably, mainly since they are both defined by a person's interpretation of an event or events. Both stress and trauma share similarities: they can involve emotional or psychological distress, impact physical health, and lead to anxiety or mood-related issues. While coping strategies may help manage both, trauma often requires more specialized care. Without appropriate support, the effects of either can be long-lasting.

While I occasionally use the terms stress and trauma interchangeably throughout this book, it's important to note that trauma carries deeper and more complex implications. As Lori Leyden (2025) explains, 'Trauma creates a dysregulation in the brain which must be addressed with physiological regulation and somatic tools for the most efficient and effective healing.' *6 These specialized approaches to healing are beyond the scope of this book. For those experiencing the effects of severe trauma, I strongly encourage seeking support from a qualified mental health professional.

What is love?

*Merriam-Webster Dictionary defines love in the following ways. 1. verb; to hold dear, cherish; 2. to like or desire actively; take pleasure in. (She **loved** to play the violin); 3. to thrive in.*

I love the first definition, which is to "hold dear" or "cherish: so you can reference that here when I speak about loving your people. Love each person on the staff in a way that shows how you hold dear and cherish that person. Does everyone act perfectly all the time? Do you? Love in a way that you want the best for them. Like parents, whether your children are human or furry, you want to treat them in a way that allows them to be their best selves and strive to ensure that you provide opportunities for success, happiness, and growth. Love is the foundation of your soul. It is love that allows one to suspend judgment of others and oneself. If we can truly love ourselves, we can suspend personalizing mean comments directed at us and hold a space for others. Love is the power we all have.

What is integrity?

The Oxford Dictionary defines this word as follows: 1. The quality of honesty and strong moral principles; moral uprightness. 2. the state of being whole and undivided.

The definition of integrity encompasses many other terms that we would also need to look up for a common understanding. As a result, I will simplify my meaning to ensure consistency in behavior across all settings, moods, and decisions. In San Bernardino, my students used to say a phrase that encapsulated this concept, which I still love to use today: *"Don't talk about it- Be about it."* This expression is the simplest and yet most profound definition of integrity. Do what you say, say what you do, and consistently express who you are and what you believe. Integrity is not always easy, especially if it conflicts with popular opinion or resistance. However, if we hold to our value of love, we can help be the best leader we can be and allow others to be their best selves.

Why should you care?

Educators across the country are experiencing burnout at unprecedented rates, with many choosing to leave the profession altogether or retreating into self-preservation, simply showing up, clocking in, and going through the motions. According to a 2022 Gallup Poll, 44% of teachers feel burned out "often" or "always." [*7] No teacher enters the profession with this mindset, but few are ever taught how to manage the stress and secondary trauma that often come simply from being in the role. Since teaching remains the primary pathway to educational leadership, most leaders have not had the opportunity to receive training in managing stress or trauma, either in themselves or in others, during their teacher preparation or administrative credential programs.

Since the pandemic, a large number of leaders have also chosen to exit the educational system. This exodus has sometimes created power vacuums, allowing the not-so-servant leader to occupy a position that can cause and create trauma. I'm confident that this occurs across every industry in varying cycles. The impact of this lack of awareness impacts millions of people every day. As passionate leaders who want to do everything in our power to create the best opportunities for the students or people we serve, we must lead the staff (including both certificated and classified personnel) in creating a loving and safe environment where everyone wants to come to our building.

When I was a high school principal, the district was short on substitutes after returning from the COVID-19 pandemic. Due to the still-rigorous regulations in California regarding COVID protocols, many schools experienced higher-than-pre-COVID absences of staff. These absences led to a district-wide issue where many classes were not covered on a daily basis. Many leaders have been in this situation at some point in their careers, so you can relate to the amount of time and energy this takes away from being an effective instructional leader. However, I didn't realize there was a problem at our school until I spoke with my eight other district high school principal colleagues. As they brought up the issue at many meetings, I went back to my team to find out if I had missed an issue that seemed so pressing to my colleagues.

My theory was that my staff were such superstars that they just handled it and went about their business (we had gone through Breakthrough Coaching, where the team was empowered to make decisions in their roles at the school). Surprisingly, when I asked my office staff, they responded that we hadn't had trouble getting substitutes and were always covered.

Upon further research, by asking the subs why they took jobs at our school, a recurring theme emerged:

everyone here treats us respectfully. (Substitutes in our district were called guest teachers and had their own union; they had many choices each day between levels, courses, and schools to choose from.) They chose our school, despite its less-than-favorable, decades-long reputation for being a tough school (all unfounded, but based on the neighborhood it was in), every day, because we treated them as family when they were on our site. This story is one example of why relationships are critical in ways we cannot predict. We must love and support our staff so that they, in turn, can love and support the students.[7]

※

This book aims to connect you with a deeper understanding of what healing leadership should be, how it manifests in schools, how it may manifest in your own life, and what you can do about it. Want to be a great leader, as referenced by many great leadership gurus like Brene Brown, Sheryl Sandberg, John Maxwell, and Stephen Covey (It's not lost on me that we have more male references in Leadership than females)? You also need to love your staff enough to give them space to heal, to improve their presence, and to do the same for your students. For those who prefer to skim for important information, highlighted subheadings throughout the book indicate key strategies or important topics in each chapter.

We know that to be an effective and influential leader in education, we need both instructional knowledge and the art and science of Leadership. While many highly qualified experts have written extensively on instructional knowledge and leadership, and I fully agree with the importance of key practices, such as prioritizing time in the classroom, this book will focus on a more nuanced aspect of leadership: the emotional well-being of educators and the role of healing in how we lead. The part you don't get in most administration programs, the part that requires you to sit with yourself, to accept criticism even when it hurts, to refrain from dismissing someone's opinion on something you have done or something that didn't go as you envisioned, and learn from it. To hurt, process, and learn, create safe spaces for everyone to do the same. Leadership is not for the faint of heart, but anyone can learn to improve their leadership skills every day.

✺

Lead & Learn Highlights

This chapter defines the terms used throughout the book, along with their denotations and connotations. The words defined in this chapter are:

* Trauma
* Stress
* Love
* Integrity

The chapter also outlined why healing leadership is so desperately needed in today's context when leading an organization.

Leadership Reflection Worksheet
Understanding Healing Leadership

As you reflect on the definitions and concepts presented in this chapter, take a moment to consider how healing leadership relates to your personal leadership journey. Use the following questions as prompts for your written reflection.

1. Did your understanding or perspective shift about any of the terms defined in this chapter (e.g., stress, trauma, regulation, resilience)? If so, how?

_____

_____

2. Which terms or ideas do you most identify with in your current leadership role, and why?

_____

_____

3. In your own words, how would you define healing leadership? Why do you believe it matters in today's educational landscape?

_____

_____

4. Reflecting on your role as a leader, what are 2–3 goals you have for yourself in applying the principles of healing leadership?

_____

_____

5. What is the first step you could take to begin leading with a healing mindset, either for yourself or your team?

_____

_____

Chapter 2

Trauma Responses in Education

"The pain of trauma can be a catalyst for personal growth, leading us to discover inner resilience we never knew we possessed."

~Judith Lewis Herman from *Trauma and Recovery*[8]

D id you know that your brain is wired to respond to stress in ways that were once essential for survival but can now impact how you lead? In this chapter, you'll explore the science behind human trauma responses and how our instinctive reactions—such as fight, flight, freeze, or fawn—are rooted in our evolutionary need to survive. You'll also have a chance to reflect on how you react under pressure and begin identifying the typical stress responses of your team members. By recognizing these patterns, you'll be better equipped to lead with empathy, awareness, and effectiveness—even in the most challenging moments.

✧

Wednesday, December 2, 2015, about 4 months into my first principalship in San Bernardino, California, chaos erupted. It was approximately two hours before the end of the day, and our on-site probation officer notified us to go on lockdown. She was slightly panicked and had very little information other than the fact that there had been a shooting at the Inland Regional Center and that the possible culprits were being pursued in the area.

Our school was about 5 miles from the center, and of course, we went on lockdown quickly. We reached out to our school's police department, which released us from lockdown about 10 minutes later. However, we were then put back on lockdown by the local San Bernardino Police Department.

This moment I had only feared and hoped would never come to fruition. Would I freeze? Would they find me curled up in a ball underneath my desk? Would I run screaming and leave leadership forever? No one knows how they will react in moments of crisis, so I was pleasantly surprised when I calmly announced over the intercom that we were safe but locked down as a precaution against outside activities.

As the end of the day drew closer, and frustrated by the back-and-forth and jurisdictional fights between the various law enforcement agencies, I fought to remain calm and hoped that nothing would come near our students. After parents began to show up at the school and bang on the door demanding their children, more fear rose in my heart. Of course, many of our staff demanded to know what was happening; some watched the news unfold, and I continued gathering as much information as possible.

As I continued to seek guidance and direction on the appropriate emergency response, our school police threw out a term I had never heard before. We were now on "lockout" but not "lockdown." Parents were told they could pick up their students, and we were supposed to operate in a quasi-lockdown.

Although this created confusion, fear, and chaos, we eventually made it through that event as the police department finally caught up with the suspected terrorists. Our students all made it home safely, and the expectation was to return the next day and resume our regular business while plans for addressing this city-wide event w*ere being discussed.*

۞

Fortunately, such incidents don't occur frequently everywhere. Unfortunately, these things do happen more frequently than we would like, as well as tragic accidents where we lose students to disease, mental health, and other tragic events like shootings. Some communities and school leaders must address it more frequently than others, prompting a different conversation about resource inequities in specific areas. In such extreme instances, many people highlight the need to address the emotional and psychological impact. Due to this visibility in extreme cases, there is increased support during those times. Crisis teams are deployed, and counselors may be available to support staff and students, as well as provide debriefing and healing opportunities for leaders.

I remember that during the *Every 15-Minute Event*, the program even brought therapy dogs. If you are not aware, *Every 15-Minutes* is a program against drunk driving sponsored by the CHP (California Highway Patrol) in collaboration with high schools around prom time. You can read more about it on their website.

When a large-scale event affects multiple people and the broader community, more attention is paid to healing the trauma of the event as people come together to support one another.

What about the other everyday events? As a leader, I underwent numerous reflections, adjustments, and release exercises to ensure I could continue to lead effectively after experiencing significant events that provided valuable lessons. But what about the less headline-grabbing, day-to-day traumas, like being a Black assistant principal in a community where students drive to school with Confederate flags on their vehicles? The steady drip of microaggressions, ineffective leadership (yes, it happens), sociopathic behavior, or the so-called "normal" parts of the job can be just as damaging over time.

※

My secretary came in and shared that there was an angry parent in the office and demanded to speak to me NOW, and if I refused to meet with her, she would go right down to the district office and complain about how I didn't keep her kid safe and that I don't care about the students. My heart jumps to my chest, and immediately, my stomach gets tied in a knot as I try to prepare for a meeting with someone guaranteed to yell at me about something I probably don't even know about.

※

The second situation is much less stressful on the body than the first, yet it occurs much more frequently and is more likely. Another example would be a student getting hurt playing basketball or 4-square or a student being unresponsive on campus, and you are unsure if they "took" something, and medical aid and parents need to be contacted.

Although these seem like small events and just a part of school leadership, these day-to-day activities have a physical impact on the body that builds up over time. Adding the political context of our work, the variety of people we encounter daily who express their own lived trauma and stress, the bureaucracy of any institution, and you have a brewing mix that, I would guess, is a significant factor in the mass exodus from education right now.

In addition to experiencing a physiological response during daily duties, we may have faced various past stresses, traumas, learned behaviors, reactions, and biases stemming from our childhood, relationships, and past or present life events. The topics in this book will remain focused on those experienced in education or those that manifest themselves through daily work with students. Just as in trauma-informed teaching, one does not need to know the cause of the trauma to be able to hold space for others' healing as a loving leader.

Now let's explore some of the stress and trauma responses that the adults show up with, in addition to everything mentioned previously that occurs just by being human in this world. I have encountered many people in my career, and one of the most common causes of stress in people's workplaces is not being seen or appreciated for the work one does. I am sure there are many reasons for that, but just as with children, some people will internalize the narrative created for them, or they may not be truly listened to, or there may be a judgment about who they are and what they produce in their workplace. Much of what follows was retrieved from the article seen in the appendix.

Humans are genetically wired for survival. Many of you reading this have likely encountered extensive discussions about the body's biological responses in a more scientifically accurate context. My goal in this section is not to explain biology (as I am definitely not qualified for that) but to create a summary of how these responses may manifest in the behavior of the people you serve.

Most of us are familiar with the essential brain layout, which functions primarily in the frontal lobe, when we feel we are in a safe space and engaged with our environment. When your brain detects that you are not secure, it moves its headquarters, if you will, to the amygdala. You are not meant to be in this state for long periods. The goal is to decrease, end, or evade danger and return to a calm, relaxed state. (WebMD)

During the move, the frontal lobe is inactive and thus cannot be used to logically and rationally analyze the world around us. This response can be caused by trauma, which we explored previously, PTSD (post-traumatic stress disorder, and chronic stress). When this happens, there are three significant sympathetic responses which date back to our ancestors' survival (and one new one): fight, flight, freeze, and a new one called fawn. The definitions and identifiers are sourced from WebMD to simplify the process.[9]

Fight

"Facing any perceived threat aggressively. When your body senses danger and believes you can overcome the threat, you'll respond in fight mode. Your brain releases signals to your body, preparing it for the physical demands of fighting." (WebMD)

I often see this in students and young people from communities with limited resources; there seems to be a comfort in handling conflict as a perceived physical threat. Overall, we start seeing this less frequently in adults in a professional setting. Instead of an all-out physical altercation (although I have interacted with some families who are still willing to be physical), this now usually manifests itself as a verbal attack. Some examples are name-calling, arguing forcefully, or other actions directed at the perceived threat. There will be physical signs of this, such as clenched fists, grinding teeth, and other similar reactions. The fight response is the easiest survival response to identify and observe when someone feels unsafe.

Is this you?

Do you respond to uncomfortable situations by having the urge to punch, kick, or stomp? Crying in anger or a tight jaw, gritting your teeth? A burning or knotted sensation in your stomach?

Flight

"The body urges you to run from danger. If your body believes you cannot overcome the danger but can avoid it by running away, you'll respond in flight mode. A surge of hormones, like adrenaline, gives your body stamina to run from danger longer than you typically could" (WebMD).

As with the previous response, the way it looks today may not be as apparent as getting up and running out of a room. Some examples of this response include excusing themselves to use the restroom when they are uncomfortable, hiding in the back of the room (or the place least likely to require engagement), and avoidance, such as always being absent during meetings or other events where they don't feel safe. This response is more difficult to identify after a single event but can be observed by examining patterns and how they respond to various stimuli.

Is this you?

Do you respond to uncomfortable situations by excessively exercising, feeling fidgety, moving legs, feet, and arms, feeling tense or trapped, and/or dilating, darting eyes?

Freeze

Your body's inability to move or act against a threat. This stress response causes you to feel immobilized. This response happens when your body doesn't think you can fight or flee.

Freeze and fawn are responses that are not definitive actions and might actually turn into fight or flight after the initial event is over and they have had a chance to move out of the initial "threat of danger." These individuals may not physically retreat, but they cannot engage at this time and often are those who say, "I need a minute," or whose face, mood, and so on, changes. This behavior can be very challenging to identify, especially in a large team, and may require follow-up conversations and trust to get them to discuss and reflect on what they felt at the moment and why. This feeling of helplessness may later lead them to avoid specific environments.

Is this you?

Do you respond to uncomfortable situations by feeling stiff, heavy, cold, numb, loud pounding, or a decreasing heart rate? Do you have a sense of dread, or did you "go pale"?

Fawn

Your body's stress response is to try to please someone and avoid conflict. This response is used after an unsuccessful attempt at fight, flight, or freeze. "The fawn response occurs primarily in people who grew up in abusive families or situations" (WebMD).

This response is a relatively new observable phenomenon that I would like to expand on, as it is less well-known. I have observed this in more people at higher levels of leadership when faced with a self-serving leader who can affect their livelihood. The threat becomes more pronounced as it intensifies. Due to the definition of fawn response, I wonder if it is an evolutionary response to trauma.

> "The fawn response often covers up distress and damage you're feeling inside due to trauma. Fawning is a common reaction to childhood abuse. The fawn response is your body's emotional reaction that involves becoming highly agreeable to the person abusing you... The fawn response is believed to occur in people who grew up

with narcissistic parents. You may have been neglected or rejected constantly as a child. Being helpful and agreeable was the only means of survival. The problem with the fawn response is that it can cause codependent adults and make you lose your sense of identity. Some other behaviors are over-dependence on the opinion of others, little to no boundaries, being easily controlled or manipulated, and vulnerability to narcissists" (WebMD, n.d.).

As a principal, I recall teachers rushing to me when I entered their classrooms to praise me or mention something they enjoyed about a previous meeting. This behavior prevented me from observing the actual instruction, which I am sure was the intent. I have heard it referred to as kissing up or other similar terms. With this definition, it is easy to spot if you are a reflective leader when a staff member can ONLY give positive comments or always agree with your ideas.

Is this you?

Do you respond to uncomfortable situations by trying to be overly helpful, being overly agreeable, and prioritizing the satisfaction of those in charge? Sometimes, they are desperate to earn your affection and appreciation, even if it means compromising your beliefs, values, and friendships.

We have all been in situations where our physical, emotional, or psychological safety is threatened. We can exhibit multiple responses depending on our growth, the situation, or other contextual factors. I grew up with many forms of abuse and had a narcissistic, sociopathic parent, but fawning was never a successful strategy for me. I exhibited a flight response for most of my life, making myself as small and hidden as possible. Over time, and in certain situations, I have demonstrated a fight-or-flight response depending on the situation. Anxiety and chronic stress can also trigger the fight or flight responses, and everyone has a different biological makeup that affects how it manifests. Fortunately, stress management is a viable option.

As I have continued to learn about leadership, I realized that my responses and understanding of others' reactions to the perception of a lack of safety are critical. I've started using these techniques (which I'll explain in detail in another chapter) to self-regulate, interrupting the cycle of reacting to others' fear responses. My goal is to create a biologically, emotionally, and psychologically safe environment for others so they, in turn, can do the same for the students we serve.

Lead & Learn Highlights

This chapter defines and provides an in-depth examination of the four survival reactions that humans display when they feel physically or psychologically unsafe. These reactions are:

* Fight
* Flight
* Freeze
* Fawn

Leadership Reflections

*Understanding Healing Leadership Through Trauma
and Survival Responses*

As a leader, recognizing trauma and survival responses, both in yourself and in others, is essential to fostering a safe and resilient environment. Use the questions below to guide your reflection and begin identifying ways to lead with greater empathy and intention.

1. What are your primary survival reactions to stress or trauma?

   _____

   _____

2. Do your reactions change depending on the situation? (e.g., community emergency, boss, parent)

   _____

   _____

3. Which survival responses have you observed among your staff or colleagues?

   _____

   _____

4. Which response—your own or others'—is the most challenging for you to manage as a leader?

_____

_____

5. How might understanding trauma and survival responses influence your leadership?

_____

_____

6. Are there specific people on your team you'll need to support more intentionally to reduce fear-based reactions?

_____

_____

7. What is your plan to create a psychologically safe environment for your team and, ultimately, for students?

_____

_____

Chapter 3

Self Awareness

"Love yourself enough to set boundaries. Your time and energy are precious. You get to choose how you use it. You teach people how to treat you by deciding what you will and won't accept."

~Anna Taylor[10]

I n this chapter, you will learn the first domain of emotional intelligence: self-awareness. It also includes reflection questions to help you start looking inward, along with strategies for identifying your own triggers. This chapter serves as the foundation of this book, providing the groundwork and basic foundation for becoming a healing leader.

⁕

My 10-year-old daughter was sitting at the table in the dining room doing math homework. Out of the blue, she started crying and saying her head hurt. I have a history of migraines, and so I assumed it was her experiencing her very first one. I gave her some medicine and put her to bed for the night. In the morning, she was still crying, sometimes screaming, and saying her head hurt and didn't eat, drink, or answer any questions her father or I had asked. We immediately took her to her pediatrician, who also agreed it may be her first migraine and prescribed her some medicine and sent us home. A few hours later, my daughter's condition had not changed.

We received a call from her doctor saying that she felt that something was off other than a migraine and that we should take her to the Loma Linda emergency room immediately. We rushed her to the hospital, where she was admitted and given a CT scan and an MRI. The doctor came back and, in one line, shattered us. "There is something in her brain." After many hours of panic and the doctors sharing with us all the possibilities of things wrong with my baby girl, she was admitted to the ICU. We found out that she had a very rare genetic abnormality called AVM in her brain that had burst, causing bleeding in the brain. She is now 24 years old, which should alleviate any stress surrounding this story. But at that time, I didn't know if I was going to lose my baby.

⁂

I was not as reflective as a new leader and thought I could separate my home or personal stresses from my work. When my 10-year-old was in the ICU, I was not functioning at my capacity at work. I had just begun my first administrative (leadership) role and was worried that missing work so soon after starting my role would be frowned upon. I tried to be strong and not let it affect the impression I made on my new bosses. But for anyone, it is impossible to walk through the door and leave a part of yourself behind. I don't even recall if I shared this part of my life with them. My husband would spend the day with her at the hospital, and I would sleep there overnight, going home in the morning to get ready for work. I didn't want to show weaknesses because I had prided myself on being the best. This whole incident took a toll I was not aware of at the time, and my body made me sick to be able to process the trauma of it all at a later time. Denial is not a healthy way to exist, nor the best way to lead people. I did not know then what I know now.

Many leadership scholars agree on the importance of leading from the inside out. Leading from the inside means that before leading others, we must first lead ourselves. Teachers, do you remember being advised to identify your triggers before your students do? That is because you can begin to manage yourself when you are self-aware. The same principles apply to healing. My learning is probably part of what led me to write this book all these years later.

Before starting my doctorate, I was fascinated by the idea of leading others and what it took to do so effectively, to be respected, and to truly make work a satisfying place where great things could be achieved. I had long before learned not to say everything on my mind when working with our customers and residents in property management. What I had not learned, however, was that my face always gave me away. My boss and mentor, Dr. Marilyn Saucedo, told me to "fix my face" numerous times when I started as VP at the high school.

She had begun her doctoral journey as a high school principal, and I was her vice principal. She was so excited that she brought the books to work and "suggested" that we read them to better our leadership. Of course, when your boss "suggests" reading something, you do it ... and I did. With that suggestion, she encouraged me to begin the doctoral journey. My dissertation and the newly discovered awareness that my face betrayed me when I experienced frustration, anger, or hurt led to research on emotional intelligence.

According to a primary researcher, Daniel Goleman (2002), this idea of being able to do four things to lead well: being aware of one's own emotions, being able to regulate those emotions, being aware of the emotions of others, and finally, regulating the feelings of others, creates one to have emotional intelligence. These skills are explored more below. However, this is where we truly begin, by starting with the self.

Identify Your Traumas, Stresses, and Reactions

As you read in Chapter 2, it is essential to be aware of your responses to trauma and stress. Be mindful of things that (even if you think you are "past it") can manifest in your leadership. These are things that can create a less-than-ideal reaction when leading others who have acted out their own trauma or in times of crisis or emergency. Think about how you grew up, your relationships with family, siblings, school interactions, power struggles, and others. Some of these stressors may be buried in your subconscious, and over time, or in some instances, circumstances may arise where you can address them (whether or not you are ready to deal with them).

Also, be aware of your stresses. These are usually not as severe, but can be detrimental if they occur frequently and persist. Many of my friends who experience microaggressions regularly start building up stress in their bodies, and it becomes a trauma to them. This effect is especially pronounced when you are in a situation where you cannot release these stresses and they accumulate. Another stressor can also be a specific type of behavior in people. Sometimes, how people act can cause anxiety when it is counter to how you are raised or is against what you have been taught, such as being socially unacceptable, rude, etc. These things must be examined objectively to reach a space where you can lead others with true grace and acceptance.

Over the years, I have been working extensively on myself. However, I still have to work through other people when dealing with people who compulsively lie and those who genuinely do not treat others with kindness (like regularly exhibiting sociopathic behaviors).

The final step is to become aware of how your body responds to stress. For me, it differs. I will hold the everyday stress in my upper back between my shoulder blades. When I deal with angry or upset people, I tend to deal with it in my stomach, and more recently, when I feel ineffective in a situation and feel suffocated, I feel it in my lungs. None of these are healthy, and I even had an incident where I was so irritated all the time that I developed heartburn so bad that I was taken to the hospital in an ambulance because the doctor thought I might be having a heart attack.

Emotional Intelligence and Daniel Goleman

I am referencing Daniel Goleman, a major contributor to the research on emotional intelligence. Although he built on previous work by many others, he is often credited for expanding it to the mainstream. I recommend a book based on his work by Travis Bradberry and Jean Greaves, who created a quiz and easy strategies to improve each area called *Emotional Intelligence 2.0*.[11] Please take the quiz in each of the five domains and explore the strategies presented. The first domain of emotional intelligence is being aware of your emotions. The best strategy is explained below, but it can be implemented in various forms, such as sharing with someone, using symbolic or artistic expression, or internal thought. The important thing is to do the reflection.

Journaling

This practice (which I included in the reflection section) may help you identify your genuine emotions, which may lead you to a profound realization about your trauma and self-worth and highlight what you genuinely need to work on. When we first encounter an event, we usually say things like "that person made me mad" as if we are on a string and they are pulling the strings as they see fit to elicit an active response from us. Over time, I have realized a few things:

1. People are often too wrapped up in their own experiences to spend energy "making" others feel some way.
2. You and only you are responsible for how you feel.
   How you feel is the narrative story you tell yourself about other people's behavior. In other words, the event or incident exists until you create a story that applies meaning to it.

That is why no one reacts the same to the same event. This deeply personal work is also how great leaders become great. They understand their internal dialogue, which affects how they create meaning. They can become curious about what people do, rather than assigning a value that may or may not be there. So, the more self-aware a leader is, the better they can show up for the people they lead and support them in their healing journey.

Lead & Learn Highlights

This chapter delves into your personal being to help you become aware of the triggers, traumas, and stressors you bring with you everywhere you go.

The next chapter will provide strategies for managing your emotional reactions to these triggers.

Leadership Reflections

Understanding Stressors

Below, list your stressors and how they affect your body or health. They can be behaviors or events that prompt a physiological response. One trigger or stressor for me is people lying outright (either to me, about me, or in a public setting, such as a board meeting).

Stressor: _____

_____

Reaction in the body: _____

_____

Stressor: _____

_____

Reaction in the body: _____

_____

Stressor: _____

_____

Reaction in the body: _____

_____

Leadership Reflections

Understanding Self-Awareness

Take some time to sit with yourself and really dig into your triggers. As you reflect, use the questions below to guide your thinking. This will be an opportunity to practice the skill of journaling. Journaling during or immediately following an intense emotional response to an event is most effective.

1. Now think of a time when you were outraged/mad/sad, whichever you would like to focus on. Journal that event here. Write about the incident and explore how you truly feel. Were you outraged? Embarrassed? Disrespected? Humiliated? Other?

2. Now, keep writing and keep asking why? Why did that make me feel a certain way? Keep asking why until it touches on a core belief or value (that's when the break-through happens).

3. Now, think of other times when you have felt this way. What was the cause? Are there patterns or multiple things? This list will give you your triggers.

4. How might knowing your triggers and reactions help you move from reaction to intentional response?

Chapter 4

Managing Your Emotional State

"But feelings can't be ignored, no matter how unjust or ungrateful they seem."

~Anne Frank[12]

"I don't want to be at the mercy of my emotions. I want to use them, to enjoy them, and to dominate them."

~Oscar Wilde[13]

In this chapter, you will learn about the second domain of emotional intelligence: self-management, which involves strategies to regulate your emotional state and increase the time between an event and your response, allowing for more intentional action.

※

I was supervising an after-school game when I received a call that one of my students had been hit by a car on the way home from school, while crossing a very busy street to FaceTime one of his friends (another student). He was rushed to the hospital, and we didn't know how he was. We eventually learned that the student had died, going through the person's windshield.

Unfortunately, the event wasn't nearly as traumatic as the aftermath, which required attention to ensure the wellness of the staff and the other students. This student had been in a small special education class setting, and one of his classmates had been on the phone call when the incident occurred. Additionally, his teachers all knew him, and he was very young for a freshman in high school.

We had a person in a position at each high school focused on supporting families in all kinds of need, which also meant we were part of planning his funeral service. The family decided on an open-casket funeral. As his principal, of course, I was expected to attend. When I showed up, the father was drunk in the parking lot, crying and repeating that he just wanted to remember his son as he was and couldn't bring himself to go into the service.

In contrast, as I entered the room with our student, his mom was right next to the casket, holding on to the edge and not ready to say goodbye to her baby. The room was full of his teachers, his girlfriend, and many of his class-mates. The whole thing broke my heart. When it was time to pay my respects, I had to approach the casket of my now-former student.

※

At that moment, it took everything I had to show compassion to his mom as a mother and not let my fears, sadness, and former trauma ruin the opportunity to show up for others. This situation was an opportunity to demonstrate Goleman's second domain of regulating one's own emotions. The first step of regulating emotions is identifying them, so I started with that in this section.

Make no mistake, the first step is not a weak or easy thing to do. When I started this process, I realized I wanted to matter. That revelation gave me tears, shoulder-shaking tears for a while before reflecting on the trauma in my life that created such a yearning to matter to others.

The next step is determining what to do when we find ourselves in highly emotional or high-stakes situations at work. Research indicates that various factors contribute to regulating your emotions, and the following is a sample of a few.

Breathing Techniques

Breathing techniques are one of my favorites, as evolution creates a fight, flight, or freeze response, which also tends to shallow breathing, reducing the amount of oxygen that flows through the body. Some common ones are just timing your inhale and exhale. My favorite is breathing in for a count of four and breathing out for a count of eight. Another common one in schools is to smell the roses and blow out the candles. Repeating this over and over until the anxiety leaves or until you have to speak to someone. If you are interested in more research on breathing, search for the vagus nerve and exercises to reset it.

Gratitude Walks

If you're at a school site consider hanging out with the kids during recess or lunch for the best experience. Just be present and talk to the kids about their day. I love to ask the kids how we could improve a school or how their classes, sports, etc., are going.

If students are not in session, such as during holidays or if you are at home, another practice is just to go outside. Walk around, noticing everything about nature: how the trees are swaying, how the heat or cold feels on your skin, and how the air gives you oxygen as you breathe in—just notice. Just Be.

Find a Confidant

Some people are auditory processors and, therefore, need a safe person to hear them as they process their thoughts and emotions and derive solutions or a way to move forward. I am an auditory processor, especially when it comes to my emotions. It is challenging for me to articulate my emotions as I experience them intensely. I need time and opportunity to process them and assign labels and reasons, in order to have a productive conversation. Knowing that about myself allows me to create opportunities to process and then follow up.

Journaling/Write that Email

Some people need to write their thoughts and feelings and visualize them on the page. Many people, however, write with their emotions in an email to respond to their feelings, and then they hit send!!! I suggest writing that email without a recipient's name and keeping it in your draft for 24 hours. Re-read it without the emotional tone, have a friend read it, then reread it, and only after that, hit send.

Spiritual and Religious Practices

There are approximately 400,000 churches throughout the United States. Humanity has thrived in the belief that there is something greater than itself. Religious and spiritual practices also provide an opportunity to hand over things that weigh on you to a higher power. Take advantage of events, rituals, and practices that align with your beliefs.

Spend Time with Friends

Good friends will help you "take your mind off things," and more importantly, you will experience connection and joy. Spending time with friends is healthy because it establishes that your body is safe and does not need to be in a state of survival. Another concept you may want to research is co-regulating, which is a strategy for helping manage other people's emotions.

Cry

Sometimes, we need to cry. Men, women, and children all need deep eye cleaning occasionally. And it is okay. During my career, when I was in property management and working with the general public, I would cry and hand in my resignation about every six months. Luckily, I had an emotionally intelligent boss who refused to take my letters and talked me through it every single time. Some people watch Lifetime movies or sad commercials; whatever your preferred method, your body needs to release the stress, which is a great way to do it.

Travel and Take Time Off

For some, this is an added stress, but for others, exploring new places, meeting new people, and experiencing different cultures is a soul-nourishing experience. It allows for the stress to process through your body without accumulating. If you are the type of person who shudders at the thought of planes, trains, and automobiles, take some time off. Stay in bed, binge-watch whatever stream service you love, or watch all the movies in a saga, order Uber Eats, and DON'T check your emails. Whatever you decide to do, the important thing is to give your mind and body a break.

Laugh!!

This is also one of my favorites! You can actually do this while working regularly. Much of the world is amusing; it depends on how you perceive it. I was going through a difficult situation where, at first, I was constantly frustrated, sad, mad, and hurt. When I finally decided I could not keep up with these emotions if I were to be healthy, I decided to look at it with a sense of humor. I started saying things like, 'I am either in a novela, a Twilight Zone episode, or on a hidden camera,' and would laugh with those going through it with me. So many things can be funny if you look for the humor.

Additional techniques listed in the trauma article referenced in Chapter 2, posted on WebMD, are categorized by type: mental, physical, and soothing. They are listed in the article, so I have expanded upon them to provide a clearer description.

Mental Focus

Focusing on your environment is similar to gratitude walks, but you don't have to leave your current location. Just start looking around and noticing things. I often see something that makes me laugh, or things I had never noticed in a room I'm always in.

Reciting Songs, Poetry, or Affirmations

This is self-explanatory.

Playing the Alphabet Game.

I had to Google this one. Go through the alphabet one letter at a time, coming up with an item or word that starts with that letter.

Mental Calculations

Do some math!! Figure out the sale price of the item you have been dreaming about. I will also add that this is where coloring mandalas or other art on your paper during meetings can be beneficial.

Visualizing Overcoming Your Fears

Everyone will be clapping for you when you complete that presentation for the board!

Physical

Touching or holding an object: Get one of those stress balls or a fidget spinner.

Putting weight on your heels and physically connecting to the ground by removing your shoes and socks and walking in dirt, grass, sand, or water.

You can also practice "tense and release" by tensing parts of your body, starting from your forehead and working your way down to your toes one by one, slowly releasing the tension.

Soothing

Think about your happy place: A fond memory, travel spot, imaginary place, etc.

Treat yourself to something comforting or joyful: ice cream, watching Harry Potter movies—whatever brings you joy!

Repeating Coping Statements

I am scared, but it will pass. Everything always works out, and it will be okay. I am not in real danger. Remind yourself that you are safe with safety statements, such as 'I am safe,' 'I am secure,' etc.

Speaking positive statements or affirmations

My favorite is "I am living my purpose."

There is an excellent book, written by twin sisters Amelia and Emily Nagoski, that offers numerous additional techniques (although primarily geared towards women) for everyone, called *Burnout*. In addition, if you have come across Joelle Hood, Ed. D., and Thriving YOUniversity, look her up and follow her on social media. She created a company to help in various ways and now travels the country, sharing techniques and strategies across the United States.

✺

Lead & Learn Highlights

This chapter offers a range of strategies for self-management during or after high-stress or traumatic events in leadership. The strategies included are:

* Breathing Techniques
* Gratitude Walks
* Find a confidant
* Journaling or writing
* Spiritual or Religious Practices
* Spend Time with Friends
* Cry
* Travel/Take time off
* Laugh
* Mental Focus
* Reciting poetry/song lyrics
* Alphabet Game
* Visualizing
* Physical
* Soothing
* Repeating coping statements
* Speaking positive statements or affirmations

Leadership Reflections

Managing Your Emotional State

As you reflect on the variety of ways to process and manage your emotions, consider the following questions when you respond.

1. Which strategies have you already used or are using now?

   _____

   _____

2. Which one (or more) will you commit to trying?

   _____

   _____

3. What have you tried and failed at? Have you tried all of these?

   _____

   _____

4. Write down your plan for incorporating these strategies into your regular practice.

   _____

   _____

Chapter 5

Trauma: Understanding Others

"If one does not understand a person, one tends to regard him as a fool."

~Carl Jung [14]

This chapter will focus on the third domain of emotional intelligence: social awareness. You will learn what to look for and strategies to identify your team's emotional state.

This book is not political, but this story will touch on a topic to exemplify this chapter.

❈

I grew up in San Diego, near the Mexico border town of TJ (Tijuana). I also thought I was Mexican for a large portion of my life. Most of my friends had grown up in Mexico or had parents who grew up there, and I have heard many stories of families who immigrated, as well as the history of the US that led to the division of Mexico and the US, created by the border established after the Treaty of Guadalupe Hidalgo. With that context, I have always had a well-defined view on immigration. For most of my life, I had no one to contradict or even disagree with, whom I knew.

Fast forward a couple of decades to my time as a principal. I had been given numerous opportunities to build relationships with the local black community. One day, a community leader visited my office. For some reason, the topic of immigration came up. He passionately expressed his views on immigration, which were not the opposite but rather a different perspective. Now, the younger, more inexperienced me would have probably either shut down or started arguing profusely about the misinformation about immigration (especially at the Mexican border). Instead, I employed a recommended phrase: 'Tell me more.' He then shared that Black people had been forcibly removed from their homes and brought to this country against their will. Despite ongoing efforts, they still have not received equal rights. Because of this, he felt the government should prioritize addressing these injustices before focusing on families seeking to immigrate.

This moment was a major life awakening for me in leadership. I didn't change my view on immigration that day, but I had a new respect and empathy for his perspective on the issue. Suspending judgment is a way to get to know our employees better. Keep asking them to tell you more.

※

Being aware of your staff's emotional well-being is similar to being aware of how our students or our own children are. Adults are just better at hiding it. Just as teachers want students to be present and ready for their lessons each day, great leaders create effective and efficient meeting times to support them in learning or reinforcing good teaching practices. The same principles apply to adults who need to move beyond their reptilian brain to learn something new. As a leader, you cannot control anything outside of the meeting, but you can give them the opportunity to be as present as possible. Sometimes, it's things you can control, and sometimes it's the most minor things that can create chaos.

Once, I changed the procedures for requesting bulk copies. Apparently, an unofficial emergency meeting was held by teachers in the parking lot, providing a space for them to complain and discuss the decision and its impact on their daily work. I did not find out about it until a few days later when I met with my union site reps for our regularly scheduled meeting. They brought up what I had thought was a more efficient and cost-effective process. They were very angry and had made assumptions that I hated them. As we discussed it, I agreed to revert to the original method.

※

Good communication certainly makes issues easier to address, but how can you sense something if no one tells you? Many of us in education learn strategies for students and then advance in the hierarchy, only to forget to apply those same techniques to the adults within the system. Stand by the door as your teachers and staff walk in, greet them, and do a check-in. Does anyone feel off? Ask them if they are ok. Does someone avoid your eye contact that usually doesn't? Make a mental note and check in with them later. There is always an opportunity for a group check-in.

One thing my mentor, Dr. Marsden, used to do was have us share anything on our minds that would prevent us from being present. We would share with our colleagues who were sitting at our tables and then share aloud if it was something related to a district policy, a question, or a direction that required an answer. When I first started working with the school staff on this, I was worried that it would turn into a lengthy complaint session. This is similar to the feeling some teachers have about "letting go of control" in the classroom.

It started out taking longer than I would have liked, but it allowed me to clarify misunderstandings and fears, and also to understand what was on their minds, so that I could work on a solution. In addition, after making it a standing activity, there were fewer misconceptions than before, and the process took less time.

Sometimes, we can tell that other people are hurt by the comments that are made. Sarcastic jests at another's expense or yours may be a great tool for hiding hurt, embarrassment, and insecurity. Finally, there is just a general vibe. If you are attuned to people, you can sense if there is a general unrest within your team. Sometimes you know the cause of a trauma, like losing a staff member, but sometimes you don't. This is precisely why we did all the work on ourselves in the previous chapters. With a lot of practice, we can begin to identify the steps our brain takes to assess threats. The simplest way I understand how it works is this: there is an event, we assess it for threats, and then we react.

The Event

The event is any stimulus that we receive. Some examples include someone running towards you, a comment made in a large meeting, or nonverbal communication during a conversation. In and of itself, it is literally just that- an event. It is important to understand the neutrality of the event, even if many of us cannot separate the event from the "meaning" of the event. Most of the time, we feel like the event has some inherent intention, emotion, or judgment that is non-negotiable.

Let me give you an example: A teacher walks up and says, "None of what you said in the meeting made sense." Now, there are many variables about tone and non-verbal cues, but let's say that you spent an inordinate amount of time ensuring that your message was clear, gave opportunities for the staff to engage in the material, and you feel like this teacher loved the previous leader, so naturally, you may feel defensive. The point here, however, is that everything following the statement "none of what you said in the meeting made sense" is your own interpretation of the event. The statement is just that, and our interpretation relies on many, many assumptions, which you know are dangerous.

Interpretation

Let's continue this hypothetical example to understand how your brain processes events. Once the event occurs, it is filtered through all our past experiences, knowledge, assumptions, and biases to make sense of it and assess the threat. This is where we label things, people, and events. Things like labeling the comment as oppositional, rude, or hostile. Once we label and identify if it is a threat to physical, emotional, or psychological well-being, we then react.

Respond Instead of React

Using all the information our brain has given us, we then react. If we deem something a threat to our safety, we respond with our fight-or-flight response, which we discussed in Chapter 2.

The better you get at creating a gap between any of these stages, the better you become as a leader. When you can hold your judgment of an event to stay curious, you can ask questions about it. This allows us to respond with a conscious response instead of a survival reaction. Keeping with the previous scenario, if we ask the person, 'What part did you not understand?' And you tell yourself, 'Maybe they missed a part; did I explain it as clearly as I needed to?' This person is very direct, so their intention may not be to be rude, but rather to truly seek understanding. When we can evaluate our own assumptions about people, things, and events, it prevents so much miscommunication and damage to relationships.

We must also remember that people perceive the world through the lens of their own experiences, knowledge, assumptions, and biases and recognizing this is a crucial step in breaking the cycle. Another opportunity to create a gap is between judgment and reaction. When we feel triggered and start to react, noticing the physical signals in our bodies can help us regulate ourselves. This allows us to return to the frontal cortex and engage in the 'stay curious' exercise. The best explanation of this phenomenon I have heard (but I cannot recall from where, but I do not take credit for this) is when we are driving, and someone cuts us off, "driving like a madman." The original, unreflective person may resort to some name-calling and angry rumblings about their irresponsible behavior.

Instead, stay curious. Ask things like I wonder if they have a woman ready to give birth in the car and need to make it to the hospital or if there is someone injured. This shifts the judgment and, as a result, your reaction to it. If you want to get really creative, you can imagine they are in a movie where they have to keep going at a certain speed so they don't trigger a bomb or something. You may never know the answers to your questions about why that person is driving too fast and too recklessly, but the intent of the activity is to practice pausing judgment and reactions to events. It seems so simple, but it is in no way easy!

Once you pause, set aside your judgments, and hold that space of curiosity, you can start to understand others.

Dr. Travis Bradberry and Dr. Jean Greaves' book, *Emotional Intelligence 2.0* (2009), based on Daniel Goleman's framework on emotional intelligence, defines social awareness as "your ability to accurately pick up on emotions in other people *and* understand what is really going on with them. This often means perceiving what other people are thinking and feeling, even if you do not feel the same way." They mention stopping the monologue in your head. This is a concise version of what we described earlier: metacognition that involves being aware of our own thinking while trying to understand what another person is thinking and feeling, thereby slowing down a process that often feels instantaneous. It is very Matrix-y.

How can we be socially aware? Below are some strategies for increasing your social awareness. Some of these are ones I have personally employed, and some are from Emotional Intelligence 2.0; however, this is not an exhaustive list. For more information, I suggest reading the book and others, such as "How to Analyze People" by Edward Benedict (2019), which focuses on nonverbal communication.

First Things First: Get to Know Your Teams

Make it a priority to intentionally get to know your team members. This starts with learning and using their names and greeting them during interactions. I've always found names challenging to remember, but I learn best when I use multiple modalities—seeing their name written, recognizing their face, and sharing a meaningful connection, like a conversation outside a football game about their background in sports. I have found that book clubs and book reads have been a fantastic way to get to know your team members differently, such as through leadership inventories or personality types. Check-ins with funny dog faces, or you can create your own and have your team choose one as a check-in, describing why they are in that picture. All of these get at the basics of getting to know an individual as a person.

Observe

Watch and listen to what people say and observe their actions. This includes body language, facial expressions, and tone of voice. Once you are practiced and truly know people, you can discern when there is discord between what people say and what they are feeling. To practice, go people-watching. Live in the moment at meetings by practicing the art of listening to be fully present. One suggestion: if you really need practice and don't want to start on real people, start at the movies. Watch characters demonstrate a range of facial expressions, tones, moods, and various forms of nonverbal communication. This is an ideal "sandbox" learning opportunity for this skill.

Body Language

Pay attention to posture, eye movement, hand gestures, and facial expressions.

Live in the Moment

We are often plagued by the past or thinking about the future. Some of us have ADD or severe ADHD, which makes it challenging to stay in the moment. One trick I use is to make it a game in my head to observe every movement of the person, sometimes even the movement of their lips, as I hear the words. The task is to stay present and hold off on judgments, etc, while the interaction is taking place.

The Art of Listening

Similar to being present, this requires focused attention. Sometimes, it's as simple as putting your phone on its side so you can't see any texts or other notifications come through while you're speaking with someone and not responding to emails while you're on the phone. In this day and age, where interruptions are a constant, this helps you truly read the person's emotional state in addition to their words. This also may pertain to taking notes during meetings. If you need the information, please write it down. However, if you have a staff member who can take notes for you, you can truly focus on listening and watching.

Ask

Asking requires a certain level of trust or a pre-existing relationship. If you are ever curious about what someone means when they say something, ask them. By staying curious, I have often learned that my initial assumption about the intent or reason behind a statement is incorrect. This allowed me not only to avoid miscommunication in that instance but also to engage more meaningfully with that person in the future.

Identify Lookouts

This is particularly necessary when you are in a new space and are building a new or large team. Before you gain widespread trust (which takes time), build a couple of relationships, such as with your leadership team, AVID team, or another group that allows team members to get close to you. Then ask them about the "parking lot" conversations, such as meetings, professional development, policies, etc. Before people feel safe, they will talk about you before school, after school, over drinks or in the parking lot. This is when you can learn the most about the social-emotional state of your team. You can use this to build additional trust by addressing misinformation or reassuring anxiety about things when you come together.

Timing and Questions

Emotional Intelligence 2.0 (2009) states that "The goal is to ask the right questions at the right time with the right frame of mind, with your audience in mind." *15 This means that even if you need information, make sure the timing is right and that by asking the question, you don't jeopardize the relationship. An example would be if someone comes up to you, tears in their eyes, to tell you about something personal they are having to deal with and need time off. In this situation, it would not be the time to ask about their attendance not being submitted on time.

Lead & Learn Highlights

This chapter explains the brain process and your ability to break the cycle of reaction, shifting it to an intentional response with practice. It defined social awareness and provided the following strategies to identify the emotional state of your team. These strategies are:

* Get to know your team
* Observe
* Body Language
* Live in the moment
* The art of listening
* Ask
* Identify Lookouts
* Timing and questions

Leadership Reflections

Trauma: Understanding Others

As you reflect on the strategies provided, consider these questions as you journal.

1. Which strategies have you already used or are using now? Which are your favorites?

    _____

    _____

2. Which one (or more) will you commit to trying?

    _____

    _____

3. Are there others that are not listed that you use?

    _____

    _____

4. Would your staff say you are in tune with their feelings about things?

    _____

    _____

5. Do you have lookouts (who are they)?

    _____

    _____

6. If this is an area to work on, what strategy or strategies will you try within a month? Journal here on how it goes.

    _____

    _____

Chapter 6

Managing Relationships

"Relationship management is your ability to use your awareness of your own emotions and those of others to manage interactions successfully."

~Travis Bradberry[16]

I n this chapter, you will learn the final domain of emotional intelligence: social management. You will learn what to look for and strategies for responding when your team members may be exhibiting survival responses or trauma symptoms.

❈

It was my first year as a principal, and I had a list of teachers to evaluate, as required by the California Department of Education. The code adheres to the process outlined in the bargaining agreement. As I was new, I began building relationships and trust with the new team. Granted, this staff endured significant lasting hurts and traumas for various reasons. Regardless of whether I had built that trust, I had to adhere to the collective bargaining deadlines. So, I entered a teacher's classroom and typed exactly what I observed. This part of the evaluation contained no subjective content since it was a transcript without commentary on what I observed during the lesson. According to the contract, I was required to email her the observation notes before the evaluation meeting, where a discussion about the lesson would take place. I emailed it immediately following the lesson.

A couple of days later, I woke up to a lengthy, five-page email from the teacher. The email was written in a furious and defensive tone, accusing me of having no integrity and only "looking for issues" in her classroom. This response took me aback. She picked apart every portion of the description by narrating how I was subjective in my observations. I did NOT respond to this email except "Let's meet."

She requested that a union representative be present at the evaluation meeting. I knew this would be a make-or-break moment for my relationship with her for the duration of my principalship, which ultimately lasted 7 years. We met, we discussed the evaluation, and I used all the strategies I knew to maximize the opportunity to build this relationship. However, this could have had a different ending if it hadn't been handled from a place of healing.

☼

We left that meeting with a better understanding of what both of us wanted for our kids. I also learned a great deal about the trauma this teacher experienced during previous administrations and how evaluations were utilized. They applied that experience and their fear of what I would "do to them" to the new situation with me. It was not personal; it was their trauma. We worked together through several situations in the future, and I know we were successful because of our ability to be aware of and manage relationships. This chapter is where the rubber meets the road.

Relationships are the focus of most books, leadership development programs, training, and other resources. Leading people requires the ability to manage relationships; every level of leadership requires this skill. Since it is so important, why did I make you read four chapters before getting to this one? Because all the pre-work needed for this, well, comes first. One of the most important yet challenging tasks is to learn about yourself, heal yourself, and understand others to manage relationships effectively. In short, get rid of your ego. The problem is that your ego does not want to go anywhere, and it pretends to want to protect you.

Many leaders start here and then realize that they must return and start from the inside out. In addition, as our society shifts to an "I want it now" mentality, we, as leaders, are pressured to make decisions quickly to move forward or solve problems. We want to be respected by those we lead, so we try to accommodate and then move on to the next thing we must solve. I would challenge anyone to slow down in decision-making and deliberately make this piece (managing relationships) part of the problem-solving equation.

I frustrated many of my staff by responding to a question with "It depends." The reason is that many people pose questions with limited information. For example, can a student leave campus? Well, there are many variables to consider when answering that question honestly. If I answer 'no,' I may have to make an exception to the rule, such as an IEP or medical reason, allowing them to leave. If I answer yes without context, there is too much room for misunderstanding between that teacher and other students. In either scenario, taking time afterward to mitigate any damage caused by my response is better spent at the front end, to understand and answer completely and contextually. This process also provides an opportunity to manage the relationship with the person asking the question, allowing you to determine the source of the inquiry (whether it is a question from a student or something more contentious).

Another quote Dr. Dale Marsden used is, "Decisions need to be made by those affected by the decision." Although this is not always possible, such as in emergencies, it should be considered when making changes, especially those that require extreme changes and mindset shifts. As much as possible, although it slows the process, the process is more effective when we involve various members of our school, district, or company community. In short, whoever will be affected by the change. Another favorite quote he said was that the leader was to be the thermostat, not the thermometer. Therefore, we should control the energy or temperature of the room, rather than reacting to the energy brought to us. For example, when dealing with an upset parent, we regulate our emotions by remaining cool, calm, and collected, rather than meeting their level of intensity. Your response to the environment or event will eventually change the emotional temperature of the space.

I also learned, during my journey with Dr. Marilyn Saucedo, the importance of being clear about the role of people in the decision-making process. It seems simple, but it is not often explicitly stated. Although we strive to include those who will be affected, there are several reasons why we cannot relinquish control of the decision-making process. One example is when there are clear outlines in law that determine the decision to be made, whether it is agreed upon or not, or in the event of a crisis or emergency.

I have seen so many people do this wrong with good intentions. For example, leaders want their team to feel like their input is valued, so they ask the team for "input" on a topic or decision. There is nothing wrong with this in and of itself, but let's look at the context. The leader has already made the decision and hopes that their leadership team comes to the same conclusion. This tactic creates a dangerous situation where the staff may come to a different conclusion and then be frustrated when the leader goes against what they agreed to, causing distrust and a feeling that their input is not valued. Team members are less likely to speak up and share their opinions openly in the future, which limits the team's potential for power and innovation. The outcome ends up being the exact opposite of what the leader wanted. I have been on teams where this has been the case and observed it in leadership spaces.

Dr. Saucedo communicated the decision-making process, explaining whether she made the ultimate decision and the reasoning behind it. The options were that she had to make the decision, and here is why: she needed input but still had to make the final decision, or we collectively make the decision.

This clear, authentic, and honest communication fosters trust that enables people to be their whole selves, and provides a predictable experience. Teams that do this are unstoppable.

Many of the successful strategies in relationship management have been mentioned before, but it is warranted to restate them in the context of relationship management.

Stay Curious, Not Furious

This concept was mentioned previously, and it is my favorite piece of advice. However, doing this requires the most work on our own triggers, responses, and ego. Stop when you notice yourself judging with assumptions. When you are aware of yourself reacting to someone's behavior, ask them clarifying questions: Why do you feel that way? What do you mean?; How so?; or Tell me more.

Handling Difficult Conversations

It is far easier and more enjoyable to be the positive, uplifting leader who gives praise and appreciation, which is an essential part of our role. However, another part of our role is having difficult conversations with people. Whether it is to address a major parent complaint or a violation of a primary expectation, we have various reasons for these conversations. These conversations are a critical part of managing relationships. We must love our staff enough to be honest and supportive and hopefully maintain and enhance our relationship. How do we do that? Several outstanding books provide detailed information on this topic, such as *"Crucial Conversations" and "Crucial Accountability"* by Patterson et al. Here are a couple of essential points that I learned in both customer service AND leadership roles:

Don't Avoid the Inevitable

We have to have a conversation we don't want to have. Sometimes, we think waiting will lessen the emotion, and maybe the "problem" will disappear. I know I have been guilty of this at least once. Avoiding conversations is never a good idea. If the conversation is with a parent, having them wait increases the anger, frustration, and other negative emotions, which build. Then it will take additional time to build rapport and trust, which prevents you from helping the parent effectively. You spend more time addressing the time they waited than addressing the concern.

If it involves a staff member, you lose valuable time during which the behavior may continue, and you may have a build-up of repeated behavior that affects students, their colleagues, and the community. You may also contribute to the issue by sharing your assumptions about that staff member's behavior. It is important to be aware of your own assumptions, frustrations, and feelings about the issue or employee before addressing the issue. You cannot avoid it or put it off for too long but wait until you can have a non-emotional response. I also learned that if people make a mistake and know a conversation is coming, it is nerve-racking to go to work every day and wait for that conversation to happen. So schedule it, follow the steps from the books, and get it over with.

Give Direct and Constructive Feedback

Most of us in leadership learned at some point to give a feedback sandwich, starting with a compliment, then providing feedback, and then closing with a compliment. However, we have also learned from leadership gurus to communicate clearly, these conflicting messages tend to "muddy the waters" for some of our staff. People deserve honesty and a direct purpose for the communication that we engage in. That doesn't mean we don't love people and treat them with respect. Sometimes we have to love people out of the profession, but we should do so in a way that helps people preserve their honor. Since you need all four skills to succeed here, you must also know who you are talking to and how they best receive information.

OTHER ADVICE

Don't Let That Conversation Be the End

Continue to build that relationship. Some of the strongest relationships I've built have been formed while taking time to chat with a staff member as I walk across campus, sit on a planter, or run into them. I have been told they felt appreciated because I took the time to see them and talk outside my office. Seeing students participate in extracurricular activities is great, but witnessing your staff take on roles beyond their assigned responsibilities is just as powerful. I loved chatting with our nutrition services staff and custodial staff while out and about on the campus.

Co-regulating

This strategy only works when you have regulated your emotions and are ready to be present for the other person. There is a power in co-regulation that activates a subconscious reaction known as mirroring. Co-regulation involves creating a safe space by using your breathing and intentionally adopting safe behaviors to help others perceive it as a non-dangerous environment. If you are successful, a phenomenon called mirroring will occur. I am also not opposed to using other environmental factors to help people feel safe, such as lavender scents or low upbeat music in the background. Once someone begins to feel, they will unconsciously start mirroring you, such as taking deep, slow breaths and sitting with their arms open. I sometimes take slow, deep breaths as I listen to the other person's concern or response to a question.

Be Accessible

Some people equate this to the "open-door" policy. Open-door does not mean that you have to be available for everyone at every moment; it DOES mean that staff need to know how they can gain access to you. This access differs for everyone, but ensuring your team has access to you builds trust and a sense of safety. My team knew I could be contacted via text message at any time of day, and I would respond when I was available, not when I was speaking with others. I also set open-door office hours before and after school hours when staff could "pop in" for whatever they needed.

Showing Emotions

We all have emotions that we demonstrate in different ways. The more in touch you are with yourself, the more authentic you can become. Society, overall, values authenticity. I have found that people will respond honestly to it if they see you consistently being genuine and honest about who you are, your values, and your behavior aligning with those values. Even if they disagree, they are more likely to trust and follow your leadership if they understand.

$$\ast$$

Lead & Learn Highlights

This chapter defines social management and explores the following strategies to help respond intentionally to team members in stress or trauma responses:

* Stay curious, not furious
* Have the crucial conversation with the intent to build that relationship
* Don't avoid the inevitable
* Give direct and constructive feedback
* Don't let the conversation be the end
* Co-regulating
* Be accessible
* Showing emotion

Leadership Reflections

Managing Relationships

As you reflect on the various ways to manage the emotional state of others, consider the following questions when responding.

1. Which strategies have you already used or are using now? How well are they working?

    _____

    _____

2. Which one (or more) will you commit to trying?

    _____

    _____

3. What caught your attention from this chapter that was new or a great reminder?

    _____

    _____

4. What is your plan to work on or refine managing others' emotions?

    _____

    _____

Chapter 7

Bringing it All Together

"You cannot lead others until you first lead yourself.
You can lead yourself at your best only if you invest in
yourself first.""

~ John Maxwell [17]

In this book, we started with trauma and survival responses, explored strategies to effectively become emotionally intelligent leaders in the four domains, referenced love, and reflected on our emotions, reactions, and awareness of others. This chapter provides a concise summary of each chapter, serving as a "Reader's Digest" version of the material.

Introduction: Healing Leadership

You've heard from the trenches about what resonates with people when they describe "good" leaders. Rarely was it about what they knew, but more about what they made the person feel, such as supported, trusted, valued, etc. The "soft skills" we often discuss in relation to student outcomes are the "essential skills" people seek in their leaders.

Chapter 1 Recap: The Power of Connection

Throughout this book, we defined the main terms: trauma, stress, love, and integrity. We discussed the current state of education, which requires us to transition from management to transformational leadership and from transactional to healing leadership to help re-energize the educational workforce.

There is a growing demand for workplace satisfaction among the new generations, as well as a decrease in burnout following COVID-19, in the current political and financial environments in which we work. We must unite people to galvanize them towards greatness for themselves and their kids.

Chapter 2 Recap: Trauma in Education

You learned a bit about the human biological responses to physical or psychological danger and how that may manifest in yourself or those you lead. Each of the four responses: fight, flight, freeze, or fawn, and what that looks like physically. We discussed that the reaction may also depend on the situation as we assess the appropriate strategy for survival. We also reflected on our default and how we have seen it in others so we can counter that response by creating a safe place instead of responding with our own triggered response.

Chapter 3 Recap: Start with Self-awareness

Self-awareness is the "ability to accurately perceive your own emotions in the moment and understand your tendencies across situations" (Bradberry & Greaves, 2009). You need to be aware of your responses to trauma and stress. Be mindful of things that (even if you think you are "past it") can manifest in your leadership. These are things that will create a less-than-ideal reaction when needing to lead others with their own acted-out trauma or in times of crisis or emergency. Think about how you grew up, your relationships with family, siblings, school interactions, power struggles, and others. Some of these issues may be buried over time, or in some instances, you may have the excellent opportunity to address them (whether or not you are ready to do so).

Chapter 4 Recap: Manage Yourself

Self-management "is what happens when you act or do not act" (Bradberry & Greaves, 2009). It is what happens between the gap of the incident or action and your reaction—the pause between something that happens, how we interpret it, and then respond. This gap is the opportunity to reflect before answering and processing our responses. If we feel someone is purposely trying to undermine us, what is the underlying cause?

Chapter 5 Recap: Understanding Others

Understanding others is "your ability to accurately pick up on emotions in other people and understand what is going on with them. This often means perceiving what other people are thinking and feeling, even if you do not feel the same way" (Bradberry & Greaves, 2009). One challenge with this skill is that sometimes people's behavior or verbal communication says something other than reality.

Chapter 6 Recap: Managing Relationships

Managing relationships is" your ability to use your awareness of your own emotions and those of others to manage interactions successfully" (Bradberry & Greaves, 2009). Using all the previous skills, how can we ensure that our communication is clear without interrupting good communication with others due to our lack of awareness or inability to understand others? We must share our own stories to model for others, increasing empathy and understanding.

In essence, this book highlights how great leaders are remembered for the way they make others feel, rather than just their knowledge, and much of this requires inner work to be that way for others. Awareness is needed, of such things as the power of connection, defining trauma and stress in education, and the shift from management to transformational and healing leadership. It explores the understanding of trauma responses in oneself and others, emphasizing self-awareness and self-management as essential skills for effective leadership.

Additionally, this book explores the significance of understanding others' emotions and fostering relationships through effective communication, empathy, and shared experiences. It provides opportunities for reflection as you go through each of those parts. Ultimately, the book offers strategies for cultivating a supportive and emotionally intelligent leadership approach to create a healthier and more engaged work environment. Together, these efforts help create a safe and supportive work environment—reducing turnover, fostering employee loyalty, and ultimately contributing to a stronger bottom line.

❋

Leadership Reflections

A holistic reflection on the book's content: Which chapter resonated with you the most, and what are you most excited to take with you moving forward?

Chapter 8

Other Tips for Successful Healing Leadership

"Leaders are made, not born. They are made by hard effort, which is the price which all of us must pay to achieve any goal that is worthwhile."

~Vince Lombardi[18]

This chapter is a grab bag of leadership insights, those extra tips and lessons I've picked up along the way that didn't quite fit in earlier chapters but are too valuable to leave out. Think of it as a bonus round of real-world advice worth keeping in your back pocket.

Be Authentic and Honest

Being authentic, honest, and straightforward with successes, failures, and plans is not as common as one would think. When I started as a school leader in San Bernardino, I won over the community by being honest about where we needed to improve at the school to address the needs of our students. Specifically, our black students. I created a community advisory group where we met to discuss the data and explore ways to partner and serve the students' needs.

Throughout this process, I met many religious leaders, community advocates, and other leaders, and members of non-profit organizations. One comment I received a lot was, "Thank you for being honest." That was strange to me because I assumed almost every leader was honest, with a few exceptions. After a while, I learned it was less than they had been lied to and more like the truth was downplayed or avoided. I was more open and transparent about my desire to address disparities and promote equity in our students' experiences. That is what they meant: that someone in the system was being open about the need to better serve their kids in the community. I have taken that to heart and try to lead that way in every community I serve.

Communication Processes

Have a system and process for communication. How do you disseminate information regularly? How do you contact and communicate with staff in the case of an emergency? How does the staff have access to you? Do they know what the process is? How do people communicate in an emergency, and what defines an emergency? All these questions should be able to be answered by everyone you serve.

Be Prepared for a Crisis

It is not something we ever want to think about, but with the world as it is, it is better to plan for something that never happens than to have no plan if it does. It is also much quicker to recover from the event than it is to deal with the chaos of making decisions during it. Unfortunately, I have had numerous opportunities to lead through crises. Most law enforcement or first responders will always advise you to have a plan and practice, because things can go sideways quickly without one.

Be Curious: Try to Dismiss Your Assumptions

Meet your people one-on-one, or take time to be with them. Explore why people respond the way they do. Keep asking why. Like in your reflections, people may not even understand why they got angry, embarrassed, disappointed, etc., about an event.

Ritualize Your Care

I love the quote from Rajkumari Neogy (2015), an executive on belonging, who states, "Ritualize your care and your joy."[19] We all know it won't get done if it's not on the calendar. She stresses that we put intentional time on our calendar to focus on wellness. Whether it's 15 minutes to get yourself settled each morning, meditation and/or prayer time during or after lunch, exercise time, laughter time, or nature walks, build it in!

Read Outside of Your Current Field

Practice your empathy by reading books in various fields, such as healthcare, business, non-profit organizations, associations, and other topics that interest you. Read leadership books that are grounded in these fields as well. See how many skills are transferable across our society. Several influential leaders lead churches (even if you are not religious). Look for commonalities - remember, love is *Just Damn Good Business* (Steve Farber, 2019).

Ask for Feedback

If your district doesn't have an established feedback process, such as a 360-degree survey for the team you serve, consider creating your own. Don't just ask questions that will guarantee you receive positive feedback, but rather open-ended ones that provide feedback for your growth. Be cautious; this requires you to be centered and have effective ways to process feedback about you and your leadership. Share the results with your team once you have processed them and looked for patterns. Being vulnerable is a powerful modeling opportunity to show reflection, continual learning, and willingness to listen and grow. This process is not exclusive to your staff; it also includes community members, parents, and students. Every perspective gives us another opportunity to improve and refine our practice.

Incorporate Laughter

Laughter is a powerful bonding experience. It releases endorphins, which help you feel good and maintain a positive mindset. It reduces stress hormones and lowers your heart rate and blood pressure. You want to ensure it's an appropriate time to laugh, especially during those non-emergency but stressful times when your team needs it the most, such as during a debriefing after a nearly horrible event or after an irate parent leaves.

An average person spends about a third of their life at work. As leaders, not only do we want to spend this time fulfilling our purpose of doing right by kids, but it is also our moral imperative to create an environment where everyone feels like they are a part of that journey, success, and responsibility. We should want to come to do what we do, especially when we have to bear so many of the burdens of the students we serve.

Call to Action

You have made it this far through the book. How much of it have you taken action on? Did you complete all the reflections as you went through or did you read it front to back with the plan to go back later? I challenge you to take your leadership to the next level, regardless of how emotionally intelligent you are, we can all improve. Take a moment to reflect on your most challenging skill.

Is it your awareness of your own emotional reaction to things, your ability to manage them, your awareness of others, or your ability to manage others? Do you receive feedback that can shed light on areas for improvement? Are you good at all of them, but struggle when you're in high-stress situations or when you're tired?

Whatever your answers, go back to that section of the book and choose one strategy and commit to practicing it for 30 days. Go back and journal your thoughts. Once you have mastered that one strategy, either choose another or move to another area of competency. This process will be continual as you grow as a leader, are challenged with new situations, have a different staff or hold different positions. The important thing, regardless of your choices, is to be aware and improve with every interaction compared to the one before. Happy leading!

✳

Lead & Learn Highlights

This chapter includes additional healing leadership advice and strategies that did not fit into the other chapters. These are:

* Be authentic and honest
* Communication Processes
* Prepare for a Crisis
* Stay Curious-try to dismiss assumptions
* Ritualize your care
* Read books authored by people outside your field
* Ask for feedback
* Bring in Laughter

Leadership Reflections

As you reflect on the variety of ways to process and manage your emotions, consider the following questions when you respond.

1. Which of these pieces of advice from the chapter are currently your favorite? If there were new ones, which ones are you most likely to try?

   _____

   _____

2. Start with the end in mind. What do you want people to remember about you and your leadership?

   _____

   _____

APPENDIX

Adverse Childhood Experience (ACE) Questionnaire [20]

Name: _____

Date: _____

This questionnaire will ask you some questions about events that happened during your childhood, specifically the first 18 years of your life. The information you provide by answering these questions will enable you to better understand problems that may have occurred early in your life and explore how those problems may be impacting the challenges you are experiencing today. This can be very helpful in the success of your treatment.

When you were growing up, during your first 18 years:

1. Did a parent or other adult in the household often:
    Swear at you, insult you, put you down, or humiliate you?
    Or act in a way that made you afraid that you might be physically hurt?
    Yes/No   If Yes, enter 1 _____

2. Did a parent or other adult in the household often:
    Push, grab, slap, or throw something at you?
    Or ever hit you so hard that you had marks or were injured?
    Yes/No   If Yes, enter 1 _____

3. Did an adult or person at least 5 years older than you ever:

    Touch or fondle you or have you touch their body in a sexual way?

    Or attempt or actually have oral, anal, or vaginal intercourse with you?

    Yes/No   If Yes, enter 1 _____

4. Did you often feel that:

    No one in your family loved you or thought you were important or special?

    Or your family didn't look out for each other, feel close to each other, or support each other?

    Yes/No   If Yes, enter 1 _____

5. Did you often feel that:

    You didn't have enough to eat, had to wear dirty clothes, and had no one to protect you?

    Or your parents were too drunk or high to take care of you or take you to the doctor if you needed it?

    Yes/No   If Yes, enter 1 _____

6. Were your parents ever separated or divorced?

    Yes/No   If Yes, enter 1 _____

7.   Were any of your parents or other adult caregivers:

Often pushed, grabbed, slapped, or had something thrown at them?

Or sometimes or often kicked, bitten, hit with a fist, or hit with something hard?

Or ever repeatedly hit over at least a few minutes or threatened with a gun or knife?

Yes/No   If Yes, enter 1 _____

8.   Did you live with anyone who was a problem drinker or alcoholic, or who used street drugs?

Yes/No   If Yes, enter 1 _____

9.   Was a household member depressed or mentally ill, or did a household member attempt suicide?

Yes/No   If Yes, enter 1 _____

10.   Did a household member go to prison?

Yes/No   If Yes, enter 1 _____

ACE SCORE (total "Yes" answers): _____

See below for how health professionals interpret this score.

Adverse Childhood Experiences (ACEs) a
Toxic Stress Risk Assessment Algorit

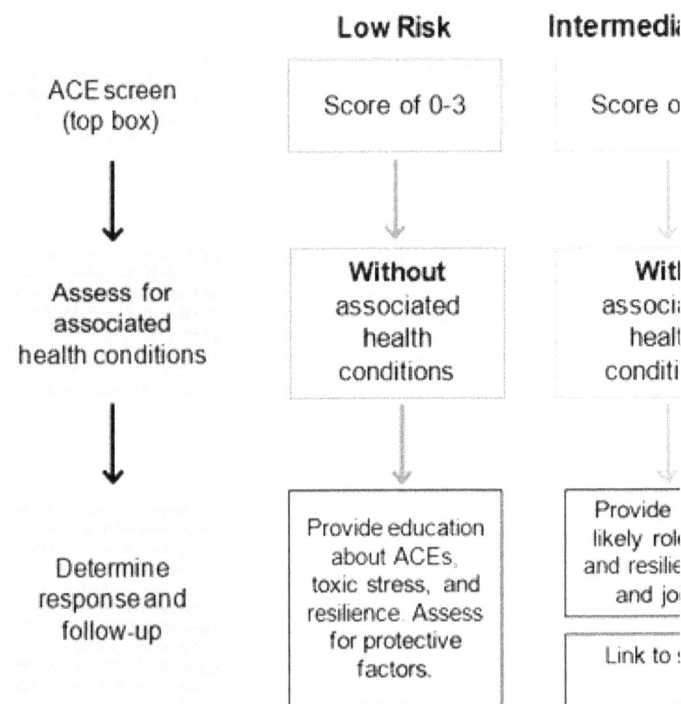

	Low Risk	**Intermedi:**
ACE screen (top box)	Score of 0-3	Score o
↓	↓	↓
Assess for associated health conditions	**Without** associated health conditions	**Witl** associ; healt conditi
↓	↓	↓
Determine response and follow-up	Provide education about ACEs, toxic stress, and resilience. Assess for protective factors.	Provide likely rol and resilie and jo
		Link to :

Partial completion may indicate discomfort or lack of understanding. If partial respons
category.

If the ACE score is 0-3 without ACE-Associated Health Conditions, the patient is at "lc
of ACEs and other adversities on health (including reviewing patient's self-assessmer
mitigate health risks. If the ACE score is 1-3 with ACE-Associated Health Conditions,
Associated Health Conditions, the patient is at "high risk" for toxic stress physiology. I
stress response and associated health conditions, as well as practices and interventio
mindfulness, mental health, and healthy relationships. The provider should also asses
services and interventions, as appropriate.

SCREEN. TREAT. HEAL.

and
·ithm

Adults

liate Risk   **High Risk**   Unknown Risk

of 1-3 | Score of 4+ | | Score unknown (incomplete) |

↓

ith
ciated
alth
itions

| **With or without** associated health conditions |

↓   ↓

e education about toxic stress, its
ble in patient's health condition(s),
lience. Assess for protective factors
jointly formulate treatment plan.

| Provide education on ACEs/toxic stress and buffering/ resilience. Re-offer at next physical. |

support services and treatment,
as appropriate.

ise indicates patient is at intermediate or high risk, follow the guidelines for that

"low risk" for toxic stress physiology. The provider should offer education on the impact
ent of ACEs' impact on health), buffering/protective factors, and interventions that can
;, the patient is at "intermediate risk." If the ACE score is 4 or higher, even without ACE-
. In both cases, the provider should offer education on how ACEs may lead to a toxic
tions demonstrated to buffer the toxic stress response, such as sleep, exercise, nutrition
ess for protective factors, jointly formulate a treatment plan and link to supportive

How Established Culture Plays a Role in Recovering from Staffing Shortages.[21]

Antoinette Gutierrez | September | October 2022

We have all used words like "unprecedented" and phrases like "learning to pivot." We have even called on previous language to describe what we all just went through during the shut-down portion of the pandemic "the recovering stage" and up to the current "new normal." Although we have faced a multitude of challenges throughout the pandemic and exposed a lot of areas in which education can improve, such as equity in resources and access, mental health and the dependence on the school system by many families, there was one that really caught us by surprise — the shortage of staffing when we returned. The excitement of returning was felt by all who had survived the time either virtually meeting or in a hybrid model with the struggle of connecting to those we could not see. As a principal, it was difficult to ensure the staff felt supported and cared for from a distance. The teachers felt the same for students who had disappeared or did not attend regularly. Staff also contended with their own families being at home and their schooling. Students, of course, craved their friends and the socialization they came to expect. Needless to say, the prospect of returning to some semblance of normalcy was palpable in all of us.

The Problem

We opened up! Along with the additional struggles of re-acclimating to the school/work schedule; COVID protocols that added a tremendous amount of work, stress, and fear; and the political environment playing out at districts and sites, we found a more immediate problem- staffing. There were so many reasons that all came together at the same time to create this perfect storm. We had COVID quarantine protocols, the fear of the health and safety of the employees themselves, the fear of being around so many people after so long, the divide of beliefs about vaccines and masks and then the normal reasons people are out, such as illness, family events, etc. We also had larger than usual amounts of death and loss across the organization.This did not affect only one group. It ranged from clerical support, special education instructional aides, teachers and other admin-istration which caused a fear that we may not even be able to continue to run. Those that were able to show up were overworked, stressed out and overwhelmed with the con-stant uncertainty.

The Silver Lining

Although the origin is unknown, there is a saying: "Necessity is the mother of all inventions." This world of unknown allowed a lot of creative solutions to be had to ensure that kids arrived each day and were served by the educational institution. Districts up and down the state had procedures where top leadership brushed off their teaching and learning credentials and jumped into the classroom to sub for teachers. We saw directors, superintendents, principals and any other district leaders getting into the trenches. Although this was a widespread initial response and solution, we all knew it was not going to last long term. Who will lead and navigate the districts and sites through this if they were in the classroom every day? The next logical solution came from human resources. Districts started looking at their resources and filling short-term and long term positions. They looked to their guest teachers (subs;, they looked to interns, alumni and community to start filling in the gaps. Different districts started looking at daily pay rates, period coverage pay for secondary and other negotiated items to try to lure substitutes to the district. We started seeing a disparity between sites within a district who were able to staff their own positions each day and ones who continued to depend on coverage from leadership. After speaking to various staff members, I discovered it was the culture of a school (possibly district) that made that huge difference.

Culture

I was principal of a comprehensive high school in a highly urban district and city. With over 50,000 students throughout the district, there were many options for people to choose where they subbed or ultimately took a position. So, not only were we in competition with other districts, but with other sites within our own. We only requested coverage from district level leadership twice. Here is why I believe that was the case:

1. **Staff didn't want to be gone.** The more consistent the staff was, the less coverage you need. It sounds so simple, but when there is a culture of love and appreciation for the work that they do, they want to come to work every day. The only absences we had when we first returned were from mandatory COVID exposure quarantines (and staff were a little bitter they were sent home).

2. **Guest teachers/subs want to come to your site.** The reputation of how you treat people or how "bad" the assignment will be definitely plays a role in whether substitutes, both certificated and classified, pick up those vacant jobs. When I first started in 2016, it was a school with a reputation of not being a good place to sub. According to one resident sub I asked this year, "the school went from a school that could hardly fill its sub positions to being one of the most sought after sub assignments. Thank you for being so supportive of the subs and making us feel like we are an integral part of the SBHS team."

3. **Building capacity and a pipeline was crucial.** We had previously been supporting our classified staff as well as the district having a "grow your own" program. During this time, we had two instructional aides who had been

working on getting their teaching credentials actually begin as intern teachers for vacant positions at our site. This was amazing for us since they knew the students, wanted to be there and had a support system already in place.

4. **Creativity was necessary.** The leadership team, and staff were strong in problem solving as well. We ended up finding student teachers who had been placed at our site who were a perfect fit for teaching positions. This helped us fill vacancies with a more permanent person, reducing the inconsistency of the daily subs. We were also able to hire student interns (former students or local students) who assisted in areas in which we were short staffed. This included technology support, clerical support or classroom support. All the while interviewing and recruiting. As a principal, it was difficult to ensure the staff felt supported and cared for from a distance. The teachers felt the same for students who had disappeared or did not attend regularly.

5. **There were structures of support for new teachers.** We had created the "New Cardinal Academy" that was a support group, training group and an overall resource for anyone new to the site. I met with them monthly to answer questions, build relationships and get them caught up on previous trainings so the whole staff had a common language and they could bond with one another. At a high school, it would have been rare for the various departments to naturally have interacted with such frequency.

This helped to increase the pride in the school and their connectedness to it which we know increases work satisfaction.

6. **Relationships helped us all get through it together.**
Teacher, admin and staff all had a high burnout rate that was sweeping the nation. With emotions and fear high throughout the country, parents and students having lost a lot of the relationships they had with the schools, there were many district depleted with resignations. Our culture (although not perfect) was one where we knew that we were all in this together and that it was a difficult time and year but it was not only us. We took one day at a time. We loved each other and held onto that.

There is no way we would have been able to weather this pandemic as well as we did, in spitc of all the struggles, if we had not already built a culture and climate of acceptance and love among the staff. And although these lessons were exacerbated because of COVID, they are essential to creating an environment for students. When the adults want to show up, it changes the experience for the students and ultimately the outcome.

References

1. Maxwell, J. C. (Year). *Healing leader: Leading yourself and others through trauma in education*. Publisher.

2. Brown, B. (2010). *The gifts of imperfection: Let go of who you think you're supposed to be and embrace who you are.* Hazelden Publishing.

3. Souers, K., & Hall, P. (2016). *Fostering resilient learners: Strategies for creating a trauma-sensitive classroom*. ASCD.

4. Collins, B. R. (2024, July 18). *3 Tips for using trauma-informed practices as a school leader*. *Edutopia*. https://www.edutopia.org/article/ trauma-informed-school-leadership-3-strategies

5. Branson, R. (n.d.). *Clients do not come first. Employees come first.* The HR Digest.

6. Leyden, L. (2025). *Trauma creates a dysregulation in the brain which must be addressed with physiological regulation and somatic tools for the most efficient and effective healing.* Retrieved June 25, 2025, from Dr. Lori Leyden's website: https://www.drlorileyden.com en.wikipedia.org

7. Gallup. (2022). Educators report the highest level of burnout among all other industries. *U.S. News & World Report*.

8. Herman, J. L. (1992). *Trauma and recovery: The aftermath of violence—from domestic abuse to political terror*. Basic Books.

9. WebMD. (2024). Acute stress response: Fight, flight, freeze, and fawn.

10. Taylor, A. (n.d.). *Love yourself enough to set boundaries. Your time and energy are precious...*Retrieved June 25, 2025, from Goodreads website: https://www.goodreads.com/ quotes/8669760-love-yourself-enough-to-set-boundaries-your-time-and-energy

11. Bradberry, T., & Greaves, J. (2009). *Emotional intelligence 2.0*. TalentSmart.

12. Frank, A. (1993). *The Diary of a Young Girl* (A. M*., Trans.; revised ed.*). Bantam Books. *(Original work published 1947)*

13. Wilde, O. (1890). *The Picture of Dorian Gray*. Lippincott's Monthly Magazine.

14. Jung, C. G. (1966). *Mysterium coniunctionis* (H. R. Hull, Trans.). Princeton University Press. (Original work published 1955)

15. Bradberry, T., & Greaves, J. (2009). *Emotional Intelligence 2.0*. TalentSmart.

16. Bradberry, T., & Greaves, J. (2009). *Emotional Intelligence 2.0*. TalentSmart. Pg. 43.

17. Maxwell, J. C. (2021). *The self-aware leader: Play to your strengths, unleash your team*. Center Street.

18. Lombardi, V. (n.d.). Leaders are made, not born. Vince Lombardi Official Website. https://www.vincelombardi. com/quotes.html

19. Neogy, R. (n.d.). *Ritualize your care and your joy.* Retrieved June 25, 2025, from iBelong/Indeed FutureWorks website https://www.indeed.com

20. Felitti, V. J., Anda, R. F., Nordenberg, D., Williamson, D. F., Spitz, A. M., Edwards, V., Koss, M. P., & Marks, J. S. (1998). *Relationship of childhood abuse and household dysfunction to many of the leading causes of death in adults: The Adverse Childhood Experiences* (ACE) Study. American Journal of Preventive Medicine, 14(4), 245–258. https://doi.org/10.1016/S0749-3797(98)00017-8

21. Gutierrez, A. (2022, September–October). *How established culture plays a role in recovering from staffing shortages.* Leadership Magazine. Association of California School Administrators.

ABOUT THE AUTHOR

With nearly two decades of leadership in education, Dr. Gutierrez has dedicated her career to fostering student success, equity, and systemic improvement. As Program Manager for Colton-Redlands-Yucaipa ROP, Dr. Gutierrez oversees Career Technical Education (CTE) programs across multiple districts, ensuring innovative learning experiences that prepare students for future success.

Previously, as Director of Multilingual Services for Coachella Valley Unified School District, she led initiatives supporting English learners, dual-language education, and migrant education, driving policy advocacy through collaborations such as DELAAN and the Long-Term English Learner Community of Practice. Her expertise extends to administrative leadership, having served as Principal of San Bernardino High School and Assistant Principal across various levels and districts, where she has strengthened curriculum development, student engagement, and instructional excellence.

Holding an Ed. D. in Organizational Leadership from Brandman University and multiple credentials from California State University, Dr. Gutierrez has cultivated expertise in change management, human dynamics, and systems leadership. Her professional development includes certifications from the National Institute of School Leaders (NISL), extensive equity training, and national coaching programs, positioning her as a thought leader in educational transformation.

Beyond her administrative roles, Dr. Gutierrez is an active voice in professional organizations such as ACSA, CALSA, CABE, and WASC, serving as a mentor, presenter, and contributor to education policy development. Their accolades include the *Equity Warrior Award*, CALSA's *Honoring Our Own* recognition, and multiple leadership awards for their impact in advancing equitable education.

A published author and featured speaker at leading conferences, Dr. Gutierrez has presented on critical topics such as community partnerships, multilingual education, and leadership development. Their research, including their dissertation on emotional intelligence in educational leadership, continues to inform best practices in school administration.

Committed to empowering students, educators, and leaders, Dr. Gutierrez remains a champion for equity, innovation, and lifelong learning in the education sector.

* 9 7 9 8 9 9 2 7 0 3 4 3 6 *